PEARSON EDEXCEL INTERNATIONAL
GCSE (9–1)

HISTORY

THE CHANGING ROLE OF INTERNATIONAL ORGANISATIONS: THE LEAGUE AND THE UN, 1919–c2011

Student Book

Georgina Blair

Series Editor: Nigel Kelly

Published by Pearson Education Limited, 80 Strand, London, WC2R 0RL.

www.pearsonglobalschools.com

Copies of official specifications for all Pearson qualifications may be found on the website: https://qualifications.pearson.com

Text © Pearson Education Limited 2017
Edited by Andrea Davison, Jane Grisdale and Juliet Gardner
Designed by Cobalt id and Pearson Education Limited
Typeset and illustrated by Phoenix Photosetting Ltd, Chatham, Kent
Original illustrations © Pearson Education Limited 2017
Cover design by Pearson Education Limited
Picture research by Andreas Schindler
Cover photo/illustration Mary Evans Picture Library: © Illustrated London News Ltd
Inside front cover Shutterstock.com: Dmitry Lobanov

The rights of Georgina Blair to be identified as author of this work have been asserted by her in accordance with the Copyright, Designs and Patents Act 1988.

First published 2017

20 19 18
10 9 8 7 6 5 4 3

British Library Cataloguing in Publication Data
A catalogue record for this book is available from the British Library

ISBN 978 0 435 18539 8

Printed in Slovakia by Neografia

Acknowledgements
The publisher would like to thank the following for their kind permission to reproduce their photographs:
(Key: b-bottom; c-centre; l-left; r-right; t-top)

Alamy Stock Photo: Allstar Picture Library 61bl, Peter Cavanagh 47br (h), Chronicle 15br, dpa picture alliance archive 53c, Everett Collection Historical 31bl, Glasshouse Images 47bc (d), Granger Historical Picture Archive 47tc (c), 47bl (b), INTERFOTO 47tl (a), 61bc, 63b, Keystone Pictures USA 47tc (e), Max McClure 54cr, Pictorial Press Ltd 31tl, The Print Collector 37c, SPUTNIK 44, 47tr (g), 48b, World History Archive 31cl, 61tl
British Cartoon Archive, University of Kent www.cartoons.ac.uk: David Low / Solo Syndication / Associated Newspapers Ltd 25bl
Getty Images: Bettmann 2, 3bl, 28br, Bernard Bisson / Sygma 104br, Corbis Historical 92tr, PASCAL GUYOT / AFP 101tr, Paul Hauf / EyeEm 88, Hulton Archive 61tr, Keystone-France / Gamma-Keystone 61br, Peter Macdiarmid 94b, George Rinhart / Corbis 22, Rolls Press / Popperfoto 74tr, SUHAILA SAHMARANI / AFP 47bc (f), Stringer / AFP 99br, RIZWAN TABASSUM / AFP 55cr, Thomas D. Mcavoy / The LIFE Picture Collection 46tr, Three Lions 68

Mary Evans Picture Library: 10tr
toonpool.com: Xavi 51c
TopFoto: 35br

All other images © Pearson Education Limited

We are grateful to the following for permission to reproduce copyright material:

Logos
Logo on page 56 International Labour Organization (ILO) with permission; Logo on page 56 with the permission of the Food and Agricultural Organization of the United Nations (FAO); Logo on page 56 from World Health Organization, with permission ; Logo on page 56 from UNICEF, with permission; Logos on page 71, page 92, page 95, page 98, page 105, page 106 from United Nations, used with permission from the United Nations.

Text
Extract on page 91 from *The Oxford Handbook on the United Nations (Oxford Handbooks in Politics & International Relations)* OUP Oxford (Weiss, T.G. and Daws,S. 2008) p.123, with permission from Oxford University Press.

Select glossary terms have been taken from *The Longman Dictionary of Contemporary English Online.*

Disclaimer
All maps in this book are drawn to support the key learning points. They are illustrative in style and are not exact representations.

Endorsement Statement
In order to ensure that this resource offers high-quality support for the associated Pearson qualification, it has been through a review process by the awarding body. This process confirms that this resource fully covers the teaching and learning content of the specification or part of a specification at which it is aimed. It also confirms that it demonstrates an appropriate balance between the development of subject skills, knowledge and understanding, in addition to preparation for assessment.

Endorsement does not cover any guidance on assessment activities or processes (e.g. practice questions or advice on how to answer assessment questions), included in the resource nor does it prescribe any particular approach to the teaching or delivery of a related course.

While the publishers have made every attempt to ensure that advice on the qualification and its assessment is accurate, the official specification and associated assessment guidance materials are the only authoritative source of information and should always be referred to for definitive guidance.

Pearson examiners have not contributed to any sections in this resource relevant to examination papers for which they have responsibility.

Examiners will not use endorsed resources as a source of material for any assessment set by Pearson. Endorsement of a resource does not mean that the resource is required to achieve this Pearson qualification, nor does it mean that it is the only suitable material available to support the qualification, and any resource lists produced by the awarding body shall include this and other appropriate resources.

ABOUT THIS BOOK

This book is written for students following the Pearson Edexcel International GCSE (9–1) History specification and covers one unit of the course. This unit is The Changing Role of International Organisations: the League and the UN, 1919–c2011, one of the Breadth Studies.

The History course has been structured so that teaching and learning can take place in any order, both in the classroom and in any independent learning. The book contains five chapters which match the five areas of content in the specification:

- The creation and successes of the League, 1919–29
- The League challenged, 1930–39
- Setting up the United Nations Organisation and its work to 1964
- The United Nations challenged, 1967–89
- The United Nations at bay, 1990–2011

Each chapter is split into multiple sections to break down content into manageable chunks and to ensure full coverage of the specification.

Each chapter features a mix of learning and activities. Sources are embedded throughout to develop your understanding and exam-style questions help you to put learning into practice. Recap pages at the end of each chapter summarise key information and let you check your understanding. Exam guidance pages help you prepare confidently for the exam.

Timeline
Visual representation of events to clarify the order in which they happened.

Learning objectives
Each section starts with a list of what you will learn in it. They are carefully tailored to address key assessment objectives central to the course.

Key term
Useful words and phrases are colour coded within the main text and picked out in the margin with concise and simple definitions. These help understanding of key subject terms and support students whose first language is not English.

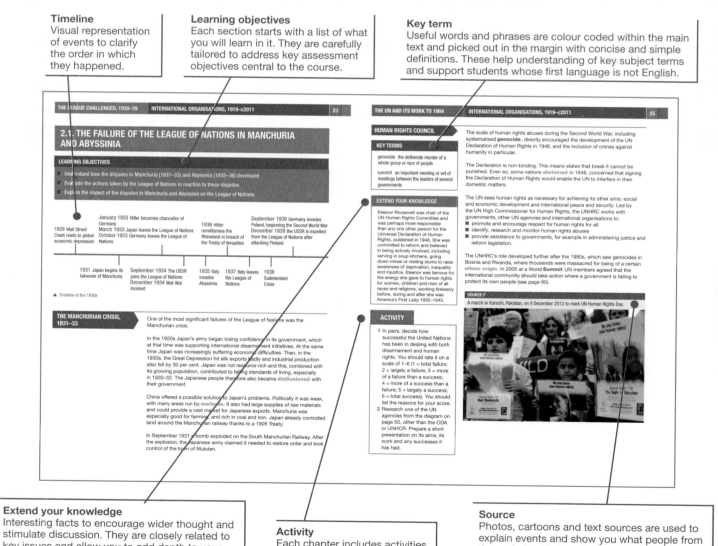

Extend your knowledge
Interesting facts to encourage wider thought and stimulate discussion. They are closely related to key issues and allow you to add depth to your knowledge and answers.

Activity
Each chapter includes activities to help check and embed knowledge and understanding.

Source
Photos, cartoons and text sources are used to explain events and show you what people from the period said, thought or created, helping you to build your understanding.

Recap
At the end of each chapter, you will find a page designed to help you consolidate and reflect on the chapter as a whole.

Recall quiz
This quick quiz is ideal for checking your knowledge or for revision.

Exam-style question
Questions tailored to the Pearson Edexcel specification to allow for practice and development of exam writing technique. They also allow for practice responding to the command words used in the exams.

Skills
Relevant exam questions have been assigned the key skills which you will gain from undertaking them, allowing for a strong focus on particular academic qualities. These transferable skills are highly valued in further study and the workplace.

Hint
All exam-style questions are accompanied by a hint to help you get started on an answer.

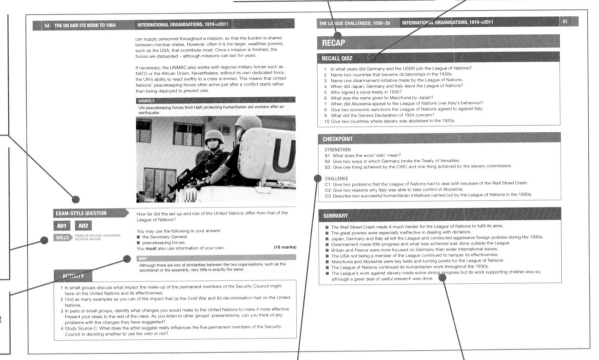

Checkpoint
Checkpoints help you to check and reflect on your learning. The Strengthen section helps you to consolidate knowledge and understanding, and check that you have grasped the basic ideas and skills. The Challenge questions push you to go beyond just understanding the information, and into evaluation and analysis of what you have studied.

Summary
The main points of each chapter are summarised in a series of bullet points. These are great for embedding core knowledge and handy for revision.

Exam guidance
At the end of each chapter, you will find two pages designed to help you better understand the exam questions and how to answer them. Each exam guidance section focuses on a particular question type that you will find in the exam, allowing you to approach them with confidence.

Student answers
Exemplar student answers are used to show what an answer to the exam question may look like. There are often two levels of answers so you can see what you need to do to write better responses.

Advice on answering the question
Three key questions about the exam question are answered here in order to explain what the question is testing and what you need to do to succeed in the exam.

Pearson Progression
Sample student answers have been given a Pearson step from 1 to 12. This tells you how well the response has met the criteria in the Pearson Progression Map.

Commentary
Feedback on the quality of the answer is provided to help you understand their strengths and weaknesses and show how they can be improved.

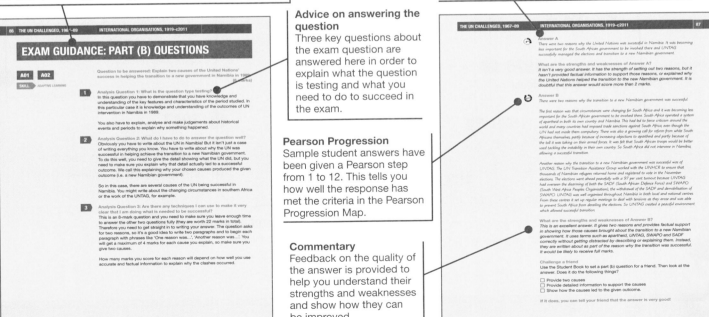

TIMELINE – INTERNATIONAL ORGANISATIONS, 1919–c2011

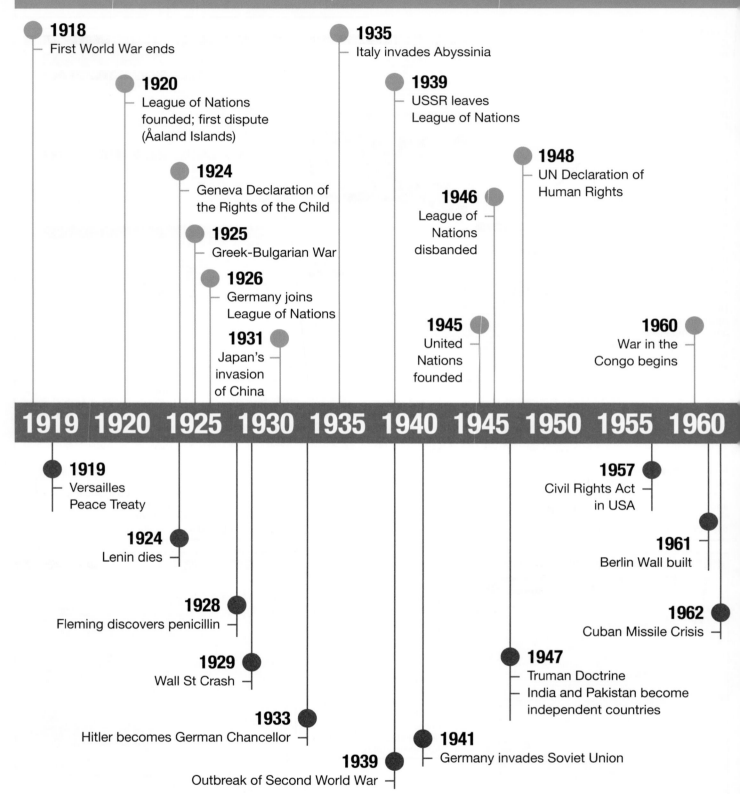

1918
First World War ends

1935
Italy invades Abyssinia

1920
League of Nations
founded; first dispute
(Åaland Islands)

1939
USSR leaves
League of Nations

1948
UN Declaration of
Human Rights

1924
Geneva Declaration of
the Rights of the Child

1946
League of
Nations
disbanded

1925
Greek-Bulgarian War

1926
Germany joins
League of Nations

1945
United
Nations
founded

1960
War in the
Congo begins

1931
Japan's
invasion
of China

1919 1920 1925 1930 1935 1940 1945 1950 1955 1960

1919
Versailles
Peace Treaty

1957
Civil Rights Act
in USA

1924
Lenin dies

1961
Berlin Wall built

1928
Fleming discovers penicillin

1929
Wall St Crash

1962
Cuban Missile Crisis

1947
Truman Doctrine
India and Pakistan become
independent countries

1933
Hitler becomes German Chancellor

1941
Germany invades Soviet Union

1939
Outbreak of Second World War

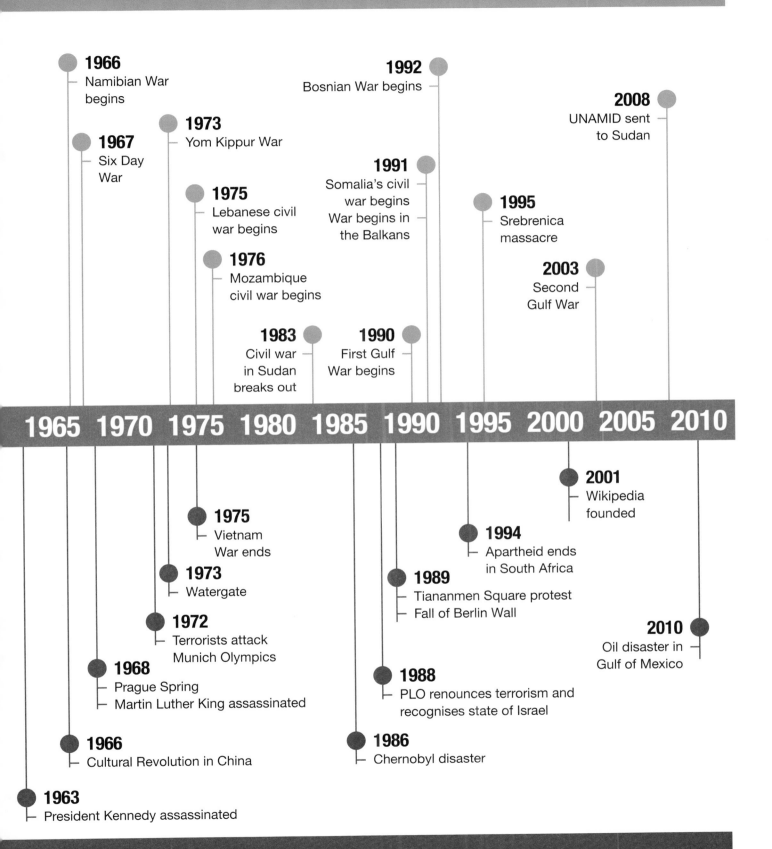

1966
Namibian War begins

1967
Six Day War

1973
Yom Kippur War

1975
Lebanese civil war begins

1976
Mozambique civil war begins

1983
Civil war in Sudan breaks out

1992
Bosnian War begins

1991
Somalia's civil war begins
War begins in the Balkans

1990
First Gulf War begins

1995
Srebrenica massacre

2003
Second Gulf War

2008
UNAMID sent to Sudan

1965 1970 1975 1980 1985 1990 1995 2000 2005 2010

1975
Vietnam War ends

1973
Watergate

1972
Terrorists attack Munich Olympics

1968
Prague Spring
Martin Luther King assassinated

1966
Cultural Revolution in China

1963
President Kennedy assassinated

1986
Chernobyl disaster

1988
PLO renounces terrorism and recognises state of Israel

1989
Tiananmen Square protest
Fall of Berlin Wall

1994
Apartheid ends in South Africa

2001
Wikipedia founded

2010
Oil disaster in Gulf of Mexico

1. THE CREATION AND SUCCESSES OF THE LEAGUE, 1919–29

LEARNING OBJECTIVES

- Explain why the League of Nations was set up
- Understand the aims and organisation of the League
- Explain and evaluate the League's strengths and weaknesses in the 1920s.

The League of Nations was created after the First World War and did not survive the Second World War. There were weaknesses in both the membership of the League of Nations and the way it was organised. This is not surprising, as it was the first time international co-operation had been tried on such a large scale. Nevertheless, in the 1920s the League was able to intervene successfully in a number of disputes between countries. There were also developments in social and humanitarian projects, such as those aimed at stopping people trafficking and helping refugees. Again, however, progress was limited by the League's weaknesses. Also, the League did not last long enough to tackle complex social and economic issues.

1.1 THE CREATION OF THE LEAGUE OF NATIONS

LEARNING OBJECTIVES

▪ Understand why the League of Nations was set up

▪ Explain the structure of the League

▪ Analyse the League's effectiveness in the 1920s.

KEY TERMS

Triple Entente alliance of countries including France, Great Britain, Russia and, from 1917, the USA

Triple Alliance alliance of countries including Austria-Hungary, Bulgaria, Germany and Turkey and the Ottoman Empire

empire group of countries controlled or ruled by another country

SOURCE A

President Woodrow Wilson of the United States.

Wars bring about great change. The First World War (1914–18) perhaps caused more change than any previous conflict in history. Although the war was focused in Europe, other countries from across the world were involved when the **Triple Entente** went to war with the **Triple Alliance**. Some of these were dragged in as parts of European **empires**.

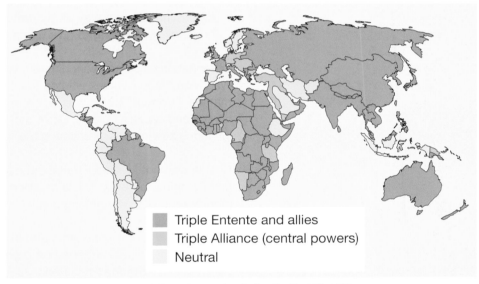

Triple Entente and allies
Triple Alliance (central powers)
Neutral

▲ Figure 1.1 Allied, Central and Neutral countries during the First World War

The damage and destruction caused by the First World War affected millions of people economically and socially. It was supposed to be the war to end all wars. Once it was over, the will to build a better world and the desire to find peaceful ways to end conflicts between nations was stronger than ever before.

The idea of an organisation of states to keep international peace had become more popular as the First World War dragged on. From early 1918, building an organisation of nations became an important aim of the Triple Entente powers, but the key person in the making of the League of Nations was US President Woodrow Wilson. After the defeat of the Triple Alliance in November 1918, a conference was set up in Versailles, Paris to discuss arrangements for post-war Europe. It was at this conference that the League of Nations was created.

PRESIDENT WILSON'S VISION

When Woodrow Wilson was representing the USA at the Paris Peace Conference, he knew that further involvement in European conflicts would not be popular with the American public. His aims, therefore, went beyond punishing the defeated powers from the First World War; he wanted lasting international peace. In January 1918 Wilson issued his famous 14 Points, outlining his vision for the post-war world.

The most important ideas contained in the 14 Points were:
- the right to **self-determination**
- **disarmament** (apart from what was necessary for a nation to protect itself)
- an end to secret **treaties** and **alliances**
- a 'League of Nations' to preserve future peace.

Although all members of the conference believed that another 'Great War' must be avoided, there were lots of different ideas on how to secure a long-lasting peace.
- France felt that its future security depended upon weakening and punishing Germany.
- Britain did not want to punish Germany too severely because that could cause more problems.
- The USA disliked **imperialism** and Wilson was passionate about self-determination as a way of guaranteeing peace. Neither Britain nor France, however, was willing to give up its empire.

Other nations also had very different issues and interests after the First World War. Many Arab peoples wanted to take control of their lands and resources now that the Ottoman Empire was defeated, and there were similar hopes across central and eastern Europe. Other nations wanted to expand their borders and influence as a means of ensuring their economic and political security.

Russia was not involved in making peace after the First World War because it had its own problems. There had been a communist revolution in 1917 and a bloody **civil war** was taking place.

With so many competing aims and interests, the post-war peace negotiations led to compromises, and the compromises led to dissatisfaction. The treaties that resulted from the Paris Peace Conference did not provide a perfect solution to the First World War. This became very clear during the interwar years (1919–39). However, the League of Nations had been created to deal with any problems and conflicts that occurred, and so keep the peace.

KEY TERMS

self-determination the right of the people of a particular region or country to govern themselves

disarmament when a country reduces its armed forces and weaponry

imperialism a system in which one country has an empire/rules others

THE COVENANT OF THE LEAGUE OF NATIONS

The **covenant** of the League of Nations:
- set out the League's aims, organisation and how it was to be run
- created the Mandates Commission to deal with the colonies taken from the German, Austro-Hungarian and Ottoman Empires
- created the Permanent International Court of Justice (PICJ) to help to settle disputes and advise on issues of international law.

THE LEAGUE OF NATIONS' AIMS

The League of Nations was born in January 1920. Article 11 of its covenant set out its most basic aim, to keep the peace between nations by:
- encouraging discussion between nations
- requiring member countries to respect other members' territorial boundaries
- working together to support a member nation attacked by an **aggressor**
- encouraging disarmament
- setting up systems to **arbitrate** disputes and take **sanctions** against nations that caused conflicts
- improving the living conditions for ordinary people through a series of **commissions**.

KEY TERM

commission a group of people whose job it is to investigate and make recommendations on a specific issue or problem

KEY TERMS

collective security an arrangement where a group of countries agrees that an attack on one of them is an attack on all of them, and that they will act together against any aggressors

peacekeeping giving support to countries as they move from war and conflict to peace

humanitarian concerned with improving bad living conditions and preventing unfair treatment of people

If disputes could not be settled by the League, **collective security** would make sure that member nations would join together against the aggressor. As the League of Nations had no military or **peacekeeping** forces of its own, however, members would have to provide any that were needed.

The commissions created by the League of Nations would carry out its wider **humanitarian** mission, which was seen as vital to maintaining world peace. People who have a good standard of living are less likely to support extremist politics or violent governments.

ACTIVITY

Write a speech as Woodrow Wilson, explaining your vision for the League of Nations. What are its aims? Why is it so important? You could research the causes of the First World War and explain in more detail how the League of Nations should prevent another war breaking out.

THE STRUCTURE OF THE LEAGUE OF NATIONS

Although international bodies and agreements had always existed, the wide-ranging aims and extensive membership of the League of Nations was an exciting new development. It wanted to deal with humanitarian issues that crossed national borders. This meant it not only needed the organisation, resources and expertise to meet its aims, it also needed to be accepted as an international authority. It would not enforce its will like an imperial power. Everything had to be done by agreement.

The League of Nations was based in Geneva, Switzerland (except the PICJ, which was at The Hague, in the Netherlands). Although all members (the Assembly) had ultimate authority over the League's actions, they only met once a year, in September. However, a smaller, decision-making group (the Council) could be called together quickly if a situation occurred. Only the secretariat and the PICJ worked all year round.

THE COUNCIL

KEY TERM

USSR (The Union of Soviet Socialist Republics) a communist nation, founded in December 1922, that covered today's Russian Federation and other states such as Latvia and Ukraine, for example. The USSR ceased to exist on 31 December 1991

The Council's main role was to settle international disputes. It held scheduled meetings four times a year until 1929 and three times a year after that. It could be called at shorter notice if necessary. This enabled the League of Nations to respond more flexibly to events. Any decisions made by the Council had to be **unanimous**.

There were four permanent members of the Council at first: France, Great Britain, Italy and Japan. Five were planned but the USA rejected League membership. Germany became the fifth when it was admitted to the League in 1926. When Germany left in 1933, its permanent seat on the Council was taken by the **USSR** when it joined in 1934. This meant that Britain and France were often the only powerful and influential countries on the Council and could forward their own interests if necessary.

THE ASSEMBLY

The Assembly was a kind of international parliament where issues affecting international peace were discussed. Every member of the League of Nations had one vote in the Assembly. All the important decisions made by the Assembly had to be agreed by the majority of members. All routine decisions had to be agreed unanimously.

The Assembly also voted on proposals made by the Council and elected the temporary nations that sat on the Council.

The Assembly's meetings were well publicised in the press around the world. This was an important part of how it operated. Public opinion in the member nations could act as an additional form of pressure on governments and **delegates**.

THE SECRETARIAT

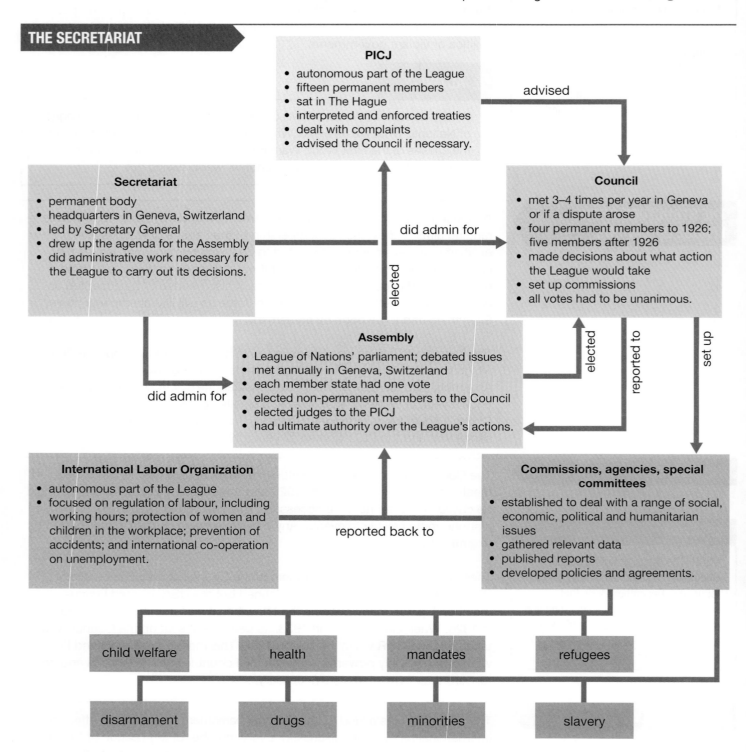

PICJ
- autonomous part of the League
- fifteen permanent members
- sat in The Hague
- interpreted and enforced treaties
- dealt with complaints
- advised the Council if necessary.

advised

Secretariat
- permanent body
- headquarters in Geneva, Switzerland
- led by Secretary General
- drew up the agenda for the Assembly
- did administrative work necessary for the League to carry out its decisions.

did admin for

elected

Council
- met 3–4 times per year in Geneva or if a dispute arose
- four permanent members to 1926; five members after 1926
- made decisions about what action the League would take
- set up commissions
- all votes had to be unanimous.

Assembly
- League of Nations' parliament; debated issues
- met annually in Geneva, Switzerland
- each member state had one vote
- elected non-permanent members to the Council
- elected judges to the PICJ
- had ultimate authority over the League's actions.

did admin for

elected   *reported to*   *set up*

International Labour Organization
- autonomous part of the League
- focused on regulation of labour, including working hours; protection of women and children in the workplace; prevention of accidents; and international co-operation on unemployment.

reported back to

Commissions, agencies, special committees
- established to deal with a range of social, economic, political and humanitarian issues
- gathered relevant data
- published reports
- developed policies and agreements.

child welfare   health   mandates   refugees

disarmament   drugs   minorities   slavery

▲ Figure 1.2 Structure and organisation of the League of Nations

People and experts from around the world worked in the Secretariat. It was an international **civil service**, headed by a Secretary General. As a permanent member of the League, the Secretary General became its **figurehead**. Although the Secretariat's role was not widely publicised, the League of Nations could not have worked without it. Its role was to investigate issues, prepare reports, translate important documents, take minutes of meetings and keep records of League activities.

MEMBERSHIP OF THE LEAGUE OF NATIONS

The membership of the League of Nations changed frequently. It increased in size during the 1920s, although some nations left (see table below) and the USA never joined.

CHANGES IN MEMBERSHIP OF THE LEAGUE OF NATIONS

DATE	NEW MEMBERS	DATE	MEMBERS LEAVING
1921	Estonia, Latvia, Lithuania	1925	Costa Rica
1922	Hungary	1926	Brazil
1923	Abyssinia (Ethiopia), Ireland	1933	Germany, Japan
1924	Dominican Republic	1935	Paraguay
1926	Germany	1936	Ethiopia, Guatemala, Honduras, Nicaragua
1931	Mexico	1937	Italy, El Salvador
1932	Iraq, Turkey	1938	Austria, Chile, Venezuela
1934	Afghanistan, Ecuador, USSR	1939	Albania, Czechoslovakia, Peru, Spain, USSR
1937	Egypt		

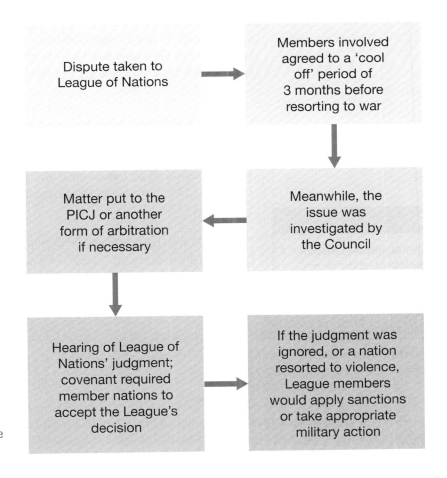

▶ **Figure 1.3** Dispute settlement in the League of Nations

NON-MEMBERS

KEY TERM

US Congress the part of the government of the USA that makes laws. It includes two elected bodies, the House of Representatives and the Senate

From the start, the membership of the League of Nations was a key weakness. When Britain and France were the only great powers on the Council, they had the most influence on the League. This enabled them to protect their own interests – for example, taking control of colonies through the Mandates Commission. Woodrow Wilson could not persuade the **US Congress** to ratify the Treaty of Versailles, nor to join the League of Nations. The American public did not want to become involved in any more European wars. The Republican Party, which supported this point of view, did very well in the 1918 American elections.

The League's effectiveness was greatly weakened by the USA not being a member.

- As the world's largest economy, the USA could have applied a great deal of economic pressure if it had threatened to cease trading with an aggressor state.
- Collective security would have been a far more powerful discouragement to aggressive countries with US involvement.
- Without the USA, Britain and France were the most powerful nations. They were imperial powers and victors in the First World War. This caused resentment and bad feeling amongst other countries, especially those that had lost the war.

Each peace treaty signed by defeated powers after the First World War included an article on the League of Nations. This did not, however, automatically make the defeated powers members, and so when the League was founded it did not include Germany, Turkey, Austria or Bulgaria. Although they joined later, the League seemed by many to have been created as a victors' club. This was especially so in Germany. The Treaty of Versailles took much of Germany's territory to create new nations and handed over its colonies to its enemies via **mandates**. Mandates were overseen by the League of Nations too.

Germany eventually joined the League of Nations in 1926. By then it had overcome many of the political and economic problems created by the war. It had also signed a new peace agreement called the Locarno Pact. It was given a permanent seat on the Council along with the four other members. After Hitler took Germany out of the League in 1933, the USSR took its place on the Council in 1934.

KEY TERMS

socialism an economic and political system in which large industries are owned by the government, and taxes are used to take some wealth away from richer citizens and give it to poorer citizens

rogue nation a nation that does not respect other states' rights and boundaries

The USSR was denied membership at first because it was communist. Communism is an extreme form of **socialism** in which the government takes over all businesses, farms and private property. According to communism the workers should run national and local government and the economy. Communists believe that workers around the world ought to rise up and overthrow their ruling classes. There were communist parties in many other countries, although most were very small. The USSR set up an organisation, Comintern, to help encourage communist **revolutions** elsewhere. As a result, the USSR was considered a dangerous, **rogue nation** and was not welcome in the League of Nations until 1934.

League of Nations

Unanimity	Membership	Victors' club	Lack of force
All decisions taken by the Council had to be unanimous. This meant that, even if action was desperately needed, one member of the Council voting against it meant it would not go ahead. The League needed full co-operation to be successful, especially as it did not have the means to enforce its decisions.	Britain and France were two of the Big Three victorious Allies, and both were imperial powers. They were also permanent members of the Council and so were involved in all key decisions. Without the USA, no other countries were as influential in the League. This caused resentment among nations that felt their interests came second to those of Britain and France.	Not all countries belonged to the League. Germany could not join until 1926 because it was a defeated country; the USSR could not join until 1934 because it was communist; the USA was never a member. All three were important international powers and their absence weakened the League.	Not having its own armed forces was an important drawback. The League was not strong enough to defend members under threat from more powerful countries, nor could it enforce its decisions. The idea of collective security became less workable as the 1930s developed.

▲ Figure 1.4 Weaknesses of the League of Nations

EXAM-STYLE QUESTION

Explain **two** causes of the weaknesses in the League of Nations' membership.   **(8 marks)**

A01   **A02**

SKILL ▸ ADAPTIVE LEARNING

HINT

Look for two problems created by the First World War (this includes the peace treaties) and explain how the League of Nations dealt with them.

EXTEND YOUR KNOWLEDGE

The Locarno Pact was signed in 1925. Germany and the countries of western Europe agreed to follow the national borders set out in the Treaty of Versailles. They also agreed to arbitration by the League of Nations if disputes between them arose. Germany then joined the League.

ACTIVITY

1 What strengths and weaknesses were there in the set-up and membership of the League of Nations?
2 How might the League of Nations approach the following issues? Which parts might be involved?
   ■ A new member wanting to join the League
   ■ An investigation into the outbreak of an epidemic
   ■ A dispute between two nations over the Treaty of Versailles
   ■ A change of non-permanent members of the Council.
3 Study Source B. What do you think the cartoonist is saying about the League?

EXTEND YOUR KNOWLEDGE

The Russian Revolution broke out in 1917 when communists overthrew the Tsar of Russia. As a result, Russia left the First World War and became known as the USSR (Union of Soviet Socialist Republics). The Tsar, his wife and five children were lined up and killed by revolutionaries. Their remains were found in a mass grave in the Ural Mountains in 1991.

SOURCE B

'The Gap in the Bridge' cartoon was published in December 1919.

THE GAP IN THE BRIDGE.

1.2 THE LEAGUE OF NATIONS AND DISPUTES IN THE 1920S

LEARNING OBJECTIVES

- Understand the disputes in which the League intervened in the 1920s
- Explain what actions the League took to settle the disputes
- Evaluate the successes and failures of the League's interventions.

Commissions were groups set up to investigate and deal with specific problems that the League of Nations wanted to do something about. Some were temporary, caused by conflicts between member states; others were long-term projects on humanitarian issues affecting people across international borders, such as health or slavery. When commissions investigated a problem they produced reports and recommendations for the Assembly to discuss. If policies were developed as a result, commissions would put those policies into practice.

The mandates and minorities commissions were especially necessary if the peace agreed after the First World War was to succeed. This was because the Treaty of Versailles had created many new nations in Europe and there was great uncertainty over the fate of the defeated powers' colonies.

▲ Figure 1.5 Map of nations before (top) and after (bottom) the Treaty of Versailles

MINORITIES COMMISSION

The Treaty of Versailles had redrawn the map of Europe, creating new states from old nations and empires. This led to national minorities being created in the new states. For example, there were large German populations in both western Poland and the Sudetenland in Czechoslovakia. The issues that such national minorities might face included protecting their culture, language or political rights.

Much of the Minorities Commission's work involved 'off the record' negotiations. These often led to more open and honest discussions, as 'off the record' means confidential, and the public were not told about them. This was done to try to gain the confidence of the countries involved in cases brought to the League.

It often proved hard to gain the confidence of the minorities themselves, however, as they disliked the secrecy involved in 'off the record' activities. Also, the minorities had to make an appeal to the League of Nations before any action could be taken, and even then nothing might happen. In fact, only 16 of the 395 petitions accepted by the League actually went to the Council to be settled. Of those, only four resulted in the national governments concerned being reprimanded. In addition, Germany, Italy and Spain had not signed the minorities' treaty and so the League could not hold them responsible for their actions.

The Minorities Commission did do a great deal of work monitoring the protection of minorities in the cases where it was put in place.

KEY TERM

autonomy the right to rule or govern oneself; being independent to make your own decisions

AALAND ISLANDS (1920)

The first dispute that the League of Nations dealt with concerned the Aaland Islands. These islands were given to Finland when it gained its independence from Russia in 1917. The population of the region was, however, 95 per cent Swedish and was concerned that its national and cultural identity would be lost under Finnish rule. The Aaland Islanders themselves campaigned for union with Sweden. Finland passed a law in May 1920 that granted them considerable **autonomy**, but the campaign continued.

In June 1920, Finland charged two campaigners with **high treason**. The dispute looked like it was getting much worse and was referred to the League of Nations.

The League proposed that the Aaland Islands would continue to belong to Finland, but also said it would guarantee that:
- the Swedish language and customs would be kept
- the appointment of the Islands' governor had to be agreed by the Islanders
- the Aaland Islands were demilitarised under the League's supervision.

▲ Figure 1.6 Disputes settled by the League of Nations in the 1920s

UPPER SILESIA (1921)

KEY TERMS

plebiscite a direct vote on a specific issue or question

lire the type of money used in Italy until 2002

compensation money paid to someone because they have suffered injury or loss, or because something they own has been damaged

The case of Upper Silesia occurred because of the redrawing of Europe's international borders after the First World War. Upper Silesia was rich in coal and industrial resources and had been part of Germany. Both the newly created Polish nation and Germany wanted it. Under the terms of the Treaty of Versailles, what happened to Upper Silesia was to be decided by **plebiscite**. This was an important example of the League's principle of self-determination.

The plebiscite, which was held in March 1921, resulted in a 54 per cent majority in favour of being part of Germany. This did not end the problem, however, because many Polish workers claimed to have been forced into voting for German rule by their German employers. In May there was an uprising and in August the issue was referred to the League of Nations.

The League's solution was to divide Upper Silesia. It gave Germany two-thirds of the territory but Poland more of the economic resources. A German–Polish co-operation commission was also established. Both sides accepted the solution.

Like the Aaland Islands, this was a success for the League. It helped that Germany was still very weak after the war and that Poland was a newly created state. When up against strong, powerful nations, the League found it more difficult to impose its decisions (see Corfu).

CORFU (1923)

EXTEND YOUR KNOWLEDGE

Mussolini saw himself as a Roman emperor, like Augustus for example, building a new empire and saving Italy from disaster. He wrote down his own legend and buried it under an obelisk in a metal box along with a medal that showed him wearing a lion skin on his head. Convinced that garlic was essential for a long life, he ate it raw in huge amounts. It was no help when he was killed by Italian rebels in 1945 and hanged upside down from a street lamp.

In 1923, five Italians were murdered on Greek soil. They had been working on redrawing the national borders between Greece and Albania as part of the First World War peace settlement. Mussolini's Italian government blamed the Greeks and attacked and invaded the island of Corfu. This was against the covenant of the League of Nations, which Italy had signed.

The Greek government brought the matter to the League of Nations. Italy was, of course, an important member of the League with a permanent seat on the Council and an ally of Britain and France. Rather than criticise the Italian government, the Council proposed that Italy withdraw from Greece, but that Greece pay 50 million **lire** as **compensation**.

Although the crisis was solved peacefully, it does also show that the League of Nations could be quite weak when dealing with major powers. Italy had clearly broken the League's covenant by attacking another member state yet, despite no evidence that the Greek government was involved in the death of the Italians, Greece had to pay Italy compensation.

THE GREEK–BULGARIAN WAR (1925)

This was another border dispute resulting from the redrawing of Europe's international boundaries after the First World War. On 19 October 1925, after a series of border incidents between Greece and Bulgaria, a small fight broke out in which two Greek border guards were killed. Suspecting that Bulgaria would attack, Greece ordered an immediate invasion. The Bulgarians responded.

The League of Nations condemned Greece and demanded both sides end their military operations. It ordered the withdrawal of all troops within 60 hours. Both sides agreed and by 29 October 1925 the incident was over. The Council did award Bulgaria 30 million Bulgarian lev (the Bulgarian currency) as compensation for Greek soldiers taking crops and cattle.

This was a success for the League of Nations. As with the Aaland Islands and Upper Silesia, it did not involve a major power. Furthermore, neither Greece nor Bulgaria had the resources to have continued a conflict, so each needed a way out.

ACTIVITY

Draw and fill in a chart with three columns to show the territorial disputes dealt with by the League of Nations in 1920, 1921 and 1925. Head the first column 'Causes', the middle one 'League's Actions' and the third one 'Outcome'.

Extension: add a fourth row to the chart and do the same for the Corfu Crisis.

Review your charts in small groups. Who were the winners and who were the losers in these disputes? You should include the League of Nations. When you have your results, discuss how fairly you think the League dealt with the disputes. Write a short paragraph summarising your conclusions.

EXAM-STYLE QUESTION

A01 **A02**

SKILL ADAPTIVE LEARNING

Explain **two** causes of the Aaland Islands dispute in 1920. **(8 marks)**

HINT
Avoid telling the story of the dispute. Explain why it happened.

1.3 THE WORK OF THE LEAGUE OF NATIONS' COMMISSIONS

LEARNING OBJECTIVES

- [ ] Explain the work undertaken by the Refugee and Drugs Commissions
- [ ] Understand the strategies used by the League in dealing with these issues
- [ ] Explain how successful the League's Refugees and Drugs Commissions were.

REFUGEE COMMISSION

KEY TERM

repatriate to send someone back to their own country

The refugee crisis after the First World War was on a scale never seen before. In addition to people displaced by the fighting, there were: over a million prisoners of war (POWs) to be **repatriated**; over a million refugees fleeing the Russian Revolution and the civil war that followed it; and thousands living in the 'wrong' country when the map of Europe was redrawn.

The refugee commission established by the League of Nations was not supposed to be permanent. Its funding was very small and its responsibility did not extend beyond Europe and the Middle East.

Norwegian Fridtjof Nansen was appointed High Commissioner for Refugees. His priority was repatriating POWs, but a number of refugee crises developed at this time as well. The largest was caused by Russia's civil war, but there were also Greeks, Bulgarians and Armenians.

DATE	CRISIS	ACTIONS TAKEN
1920–22	Repatriation of POWs after the First World War. There were also 1.5 million POWs in USSR and Russian POWs unable or unwilling to return home due to chaos of civil war.	Huge international operation to organise **funds**, shipping and resources 427,886 POWs from 26 different countries repatriated at a cost of less than £1 each
1920–25	1.5 million Russian refugees fled civil war. Huge numbers arrived in Turkey, Greece, Yugoslavia and elsewhere in Europe. International Red Cross called for League of Nations to establish a commission to deal with the problem.	Introduced identity documents for refugees (known as 'Nansen passports') Fridtjof Nansen co-ordinated 44 different nations to take Russian refugees who did not want to return to the communist USSR 1922: agreement made with the USSR to repatriate those who wanted to return home
1919–23	There was conflict between Greece and Turkey as the Ottoman Empire collapsed. Greece expanded into Turkish territory, massacring huge numbers of Turks. Turkey retook lands occupied by Greece, massacring Greeks and Armenians living there. They then set fire to Smyrna (Izmir).	Dealt with immediate care of refugees by tackling food shortages and health care problems, working with the International Red Cross and Red Crescent 1923: forced a population exchange; 1.4 million Greeks left Turkey for Greece; 400,000 Turks left Greece for Turkey Arranged loans for Greece to provide refugees with homes and farming resources – as a result of which the Greek economy became stronger
1920s–1930s	Armenian refugee crisis. Armenians suffered atrocities by the Turks during both the First World War and the Greek–Turkish conflict. Armenians did not have a home state to which to return. 45,000 fled to Greece, 90,000 to Syria and Lebanon. They lived in camps at Aleppo, Beirut and Alexandretta.	Special committee established with the International Labour Organization (ILO) in 1926 to deal with the refugees, **resettling** them and finding them work By 1938, 36,000 Armenian refugees had been resettled and found employment, leading to new **settlements** and agricultural colonies. All this helped the region as a whole
1930s	Hitler's Nazi regime persecuted German Jews, leading to waves of refugees in the 1930s.	League of Nations protected 600,000 refugees from Germany, arranging for 27,000 to resettle in Palestine; 9,000 in the USA; and 25,000 across Europe

▲ Russian refugees in Turkey

On a map of interwar Europe and the Middle East, draw arrows to show the flows of refugees. Where did they come from and go to? (Indicate those going to the USA with an arrow pointing over the Atlantic.) Add dates and numbers, if possible.

Fridtjof Nansen's approach to refugee crises was significant for two reasons.

1 His approach was to care for refugees, often working with the ILO to find them employment or settle them permanently. He accepted that although repatriation was the best option, it was not always possible.
2 Refugees did not have identity papers or passports to enable them to travel. Fridtjof Nansen introduced so-called 'Nansen passports' that were accepted by the governments of 50 different nations by 1929.

DRUGS COMMISSION

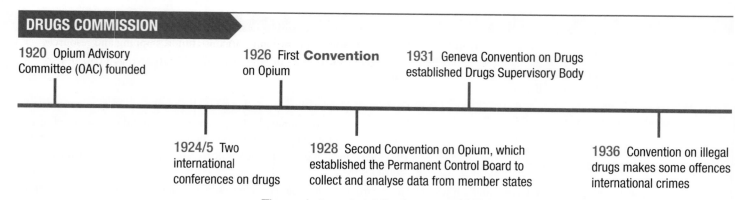

1920 Opium Advisory Committee (OAC) founded

1926 First **Convention** on Opium

1931 Geneva Convention on Drugs established Drugs Supervisory Body

1924/5 Two international conferences on drugs

1928 Second Convention on Opium, which established the Permanent Control Board to collect and analyse data from member states

1936 Convention on illegal drugs makes some offences international crimes

KEY TERM

convention a conference or meeting to discuss a particular matter

The main targets of the League of Nations' drugs commission were opium and coca. The commission started as the Permanent Central Opium Board. Opium, which is made from poppy flowers, and the coca plant can be used to make the drugs heroin, cocaine, morphine and codeine. All are highly addictive. Although there are some important medical uses for these drugs, many are grown, made, traded and used illegally around the world.

Dr. Rachel Crowdy led the League of Nations' work to deal with the problems caused by illegal drugs. The methods that were used included:

- limiting the legal production, manufacture and trade of dangerous drugs
- gathering information on the production, manufacture and trade of dangerous drugs
- monitoring the production, manufacture and trade of dangerous drugs
- finding economic alternatives for opium growing regions
- monitoring member nations' **compliance** with League of Nations agreements
- recommending an **embargo** on trading in drugs with nations not following agreements.

The OAC first focused on controlling the legal trade in drugs. By knowing which drugs were traded legally, it could then identify what trade was illegal more easily. It did this by monitoring which countries produced far more drugs made from opium and coca leaves than they needed. Then it investigated where the extra, illegal drugs were being sent.

The OAC also categorised dangerous drugs for the first time. The categories were based upon both a drug's danger and its medicinal benefits.

By the late 1930s the OAC focused more on the trade in illegal drugs, leading to some offences being made international crimes.

DRUGS: HOW SUCCESSFUL WAS THE LEAGUE OF NATIONS?

EVIDENCE OF SUCCESS	LIMITATIONS
Countries not in the League of Nations, such as the USA, often worked with it and agreed to its international conventions.	As drug companies became limited by the League's controls, more moved to countries that ignored them.
The USA reported a 50% fall in drug addicts in the 1930s.	The illegal trade in drugs was hard to control. Some countries, such as Persia (Iran), produced even more to meet the illegal demand for drugs. China also still produced opium far in excess of its legal requirements.
Data gathered by the League's OAC gave a clear picture of the supply and demand for legal drugs and also where illegal drugs were a big problem.	
By 1935 the legal production of dangerous drugs was estimated to be equal to the medical and scientific demands for them.	By the late 1930s fewer countries were co-operating. Japan, Germany and Italy, for example, had all left the League of Nations.

First Convention on Opium, 1926
- Importing, selling and distributing drugs was to be a government monopoly (except for retail sales).
- The number of retailers licensed to sell drugs was to be restricted by member countries.
- The sale and use of opium by minors was prohibited.

Second Convention on Opium, 1928
- System of import and export licenses was developed for dangerous drugs.
- The Permanent Control Board was established to collate and review data from member states.
- Nations producing more drugs than needed for legal purposes were required to provide an explanation.

1931 Convention on Drugs
- Nations agreed to estimate the quantity of drugs needed for medical and scientific purposes and to stop manufacturing or importing drugs when this limit was reached.
- A new committee, the Drugs Supervisory Body, was established to oversee international drugs requirements and estimate the needs of countries not signed up to the convention.
- Categorisation of drugs was introduced based upon their dangerous effects and medicinal benefits. Under this system, heroin was banned from export except under exceptional circumstances.

▲ **Figure 1.7** Drugs Conventions

OTHER COMMISSIONS OF THE LEAGUE OF NATIONS

The table below shows that the League of Nations commissions did have some successes. In fact, many continued after the League had ended and became part of the work of the United Nations. The United Nations International Children's Emergency Fund (UNICEF), the High Commissioner for Refugees (UNHCR) and the World Health Organization (WHO), for example, are all based on the aims, agencies and commissions of the League of Nations.

COMMISSION	ROLE	ACTIONS AND IMPACT
Disarmament	To decrease national **armaments** to what was necessary only for defence against aggressors (Article 8 of the covenant of the League of Nations)	Geneva Protocol 1924 – all signatories promised disarmament and abandoned war as a means of settling disputes (influenced Locarno Pact in 1925) World Disarmament Conference 1932
Health	To prevent spread of disease, improve access to health care To organise major health campaigns To spread information about disease and good practice To promote standardisation of medications across the world	1921 Epidemiological Intelligence Service established to provide information on infectious diseases 1923 Health Committee set up to investigate a wide range of diseases 1928 Institute for the Study of Malaria set up
International Labour Organization	Created as part of the Treaty of Versailles to deal with workers' pay, rights and working conditions	Annual conferences By 1939 67 conventions were agreed on issues such as hours, unemployment, women's and children's working conditions and health and safety
Mandates (Also see pages 4 and 8)	To monitor and govern the former colonies of the defeated powers that were not ready to be independent	Divided colonies into one of three types, depending on how ready they were for independence
Slavery	To deal with slavery, the slave trade and people trafficking	1921 Conference: agreed to tackle people trafficking in women and children 1924–26: investigated trafficking in Europe, the Mediterranean region and America 1926: convention on slavery defined slavery 1929: investigated people trafficking in the Near, Middle and Far East Also investigated slavery in Liberia, Abyssinia, Somalia, the Red Sea area, Burma, Nepal, Jordan, Persia (Iran) during 1920s and 1930s

Not all members of the League of Nations either signed up to or carried out the conventions about issues such as working hours, people trafficking or the rights of children. This is perhaps not surprising, as the League was developing new ideas through its commitment to international, humanitarian projects. National governments were not used to working with international organisations to deal with social, economic or even political problems. The disarmament commission was perhaps the most significant failure (see Chapter 2).

CONCLUSION

The 1920s was a positive decade for the new League of Nations. It dealt effectively with some of the consequences of the First World War and the Treaty of Versailles. Problems concerning refugees, minorities and border disputes, for example, were generally dealt with successfully. However, the League did not have to deal with any powerful aggressors at this time.

A lot of the League's work was complex, long term and needed international co-operation (such as health, slavery, working conditions and illegal drugs) but it made some progress. Agreeing on a definition of slavery (see table, page 17) might seem like an easy task, but different cultures had different ideas. For example, are people who work for free because they are in debt slaves?

The weaknesses in the League of Nations caused by its membership and lack of armed forces only threatened it in the 1930s. By that time the world had changed a great deal, due to the Great Depression that began in 1929. This was also the time when disarmament became both a big issue and a big failure for the League.

ACTIVITY

Work in pairs. Pick the three most successful outcomes from the League of Nations' commissions on (a) refugees and (b) drugs.

Identify the least successful outcomes from the commissions on (a) refugees and (b) drugs.

Join with another pair. Make a short presentation to show to the rest of the group comparing the work of the two commissions. Answer these three questions.
- How did the League of Nations use economic methods in addressing the problems of refugees and drugs?
- Which was more successful? You could use a six point scale. 6 = fully achieved all aims; 5 = largely successful in achieving its aims; 4 = more successful than not; 3 = failures slightly greater than successes; 2 = largely a failure; 1 = complete failure.
- Why? You must use what you have learned to provide evidence to support your answer.

Design a poster, or make a leaflet, encouraging member states to help with refugee crises. Think about how you could effectively get across your message about (a) the situation of the refugees; (b) what could be done to help them; (c) why helping refugees is important.

RECAP

RECALL QUIZ

1 Who was president of the USA at the end of the First World War?
2 When was the League of Nations founded?
3 What was the name of the document setting out the League's aims?
4 Which part of the League of Nations met three to four times a year and whenever there was an emergency?
5 What and when was the first territorial dispute settled by the League?
6 What problem was the first dealt with by the refugee commission?
7 Which drug was the original focus of the League's drugs commission?
8 Which country became the fifth permanent member of the Council in 1926?
9 Which two members of the League of Nations went to war in 1925?
10 What was the name of the first High Commissioner for Refugees?

CHECKPOINT

STRENGTHEN
S1 Name two nations that were not members of the League of Nations when it was founded in 1920.
S2 Name three commissions established by the League of Nations.
S3 What does self-determination mean?

CHALLENGE
C1 Why was the League of Nations able to settle the territorial disputes in the Aaland Islands, Upper Silesia and the Greek–Bulgarian War?
C2 Explain two ways in which the League of Nations could help to ensure peace.
C3 Give two ways in which the League of Nations could be considered groundbreaking.

SUMMARY

- The League of Nations was created by the Paris Peace Conference after the First World War.
- The most important aim of the League was to secure and maintain peace.
- All member nations attended and voted in the Assembly on the decisions made by the Council.
- The Council of the League of Nations was its decision-making body.
- A range of League of Nations commissions dealt with social, economic and humanitarian issues.
- The Permanent Court of International Justice in The Hague was founded with the League of Nations.
- The USA was not a member of the League, which proved to be a serious weakness.
- During the 1920s, the League successfully settled a number of territorial disputes.
- The League of Nations made progress in controlling the drugs trade in the 1920s and 1930s.
- The League of Nations successfully dealt with several refugee crises in the 1920s and 1930s.

EXAM GUIDANCE: PART (B) QUESTIONS

A01   **A02**

SKILL   ADAPTIVE LEARNING

Question to be answered: Explain two causes of the League of Nations' involvement with refugees.

(8 marks)

1   **Analysis Question 1: What is the question type testing?**
In this question you have to demonstrate that you have knowledge and understanding of the key features and characteristics of the period studied. In this particular case it is knowledge and understanding of why the League of Nations became involved in refugee problems.

You also have to explain, analyse and make judgements about historical events and periods to explain ways in which there were similarities between those events/periods.

2   **Analysis Question 2: What do I have to do to answer the question well?**
Obviously you have to write about the causes of the refugee problems dealt with by the League of Nations, but it isn't just a case of writing everything you know. You have to write about why there were refugee problems. To do this well, you need to give detail showing different reasons why the League was needed to deal with refugee crises. We call this explaining why your chosen causes produced the given outcome (i.e. why there were problems with refugees for the League of Nations to deal with).

In this case, there are several causes of refugee problems. You might write about the Russian civil war, atrocities against the Armenians or Russian revolution or the scale of the problems, for example.

3   **Analysis Question 3: Are there any techniques I can use to make it very clear that I am doing what is needed to be successful?**
This is an 8-mark question and you need to make sure you leave enough time to answer the other two questions fully (they are worth 22 marks in total). Therefore you need to get straight in to writing your answer. The question asks for two causes, so it's a good idea to write two paragraphs and to begin each paragraph with phrases like 'One cause was…', 'Another cause was… '. You will get a maximum of 4 marks for each cause you explain, so make sure you give two causes.

How many marks you score for each cause will depend on how well you use accurate and factual information to explain why the refugee crises occurred.

Answer A

There were two reasons why there were refugee problems for the League of Nations to deal with. One was the Russian civil war. Another was the collapse of the Ottoman Empire.

What are the strengths and weaknesses of Answer A?
It isn't a very good answer. It does give two reasons, as the question asks, but it hasn't provided factual information to support those reasons, or explained why the crises came about. It is doubtful that this answer would score more than 2 marks.

Answer B

Two reasons why there were refugee problems for the League to deal with were the Russian civil war and the collapse of the Ottoman Empire. After the Russian Revolution, civil war broke out and many Russians fled the fighting. Huge numbers of people arrived in Turkey, Greece, Yugoslavia and across Europe. The International Red Cross was unable to cope with the scale of the problem and so called on the League for help.

The collapse of the Ottoman Empire led to Greece trying to expand into Turkey and killing huge numbers of Turks. Turkey fought back and killed thousands of Greeks and Armenians. Turks, Greeks and Armenians all fled the fighting. The League was needed to help the International Red Cross and Red Crescent and to organise a population exchange between Greece and Turkey and provide loans to Greece to deal with refugees. Armenians continued to be massacred into the 1930s, so tens of thousands fled to Syria and Lebanon. The League and the ILO were needed to provide shelter and resettle them.

What are the strengths and weaknesses of Answer B?
This is an excellent answer. It gives two causes and provides factual support in showing why the League of Nations was needed to deal with refugees. The answer uses information such as why the League had to intervene in refugee problems without describing the situations in detail. The question did not require a description of events. It would be likely to receive full marks.

Challenge a friend
Use the Student Book to set a part (b) question for a friend. Then look at the answer. Does it do the following things?

☐ Provide two similarities
☐ Provide detailed information to explain why they are similarities.

If it does, you can tell your friend that the answer is very good!

2. THE LEAGUE CHALLENGED, 1930–39

LEARNING OBJECTIVES

- Understand how the circumstances in which the League of Nations operated had changed in the 1930s
- Explain why the League of Nations failed to curb Japan and Italy in the 1930s
- Understand how the League of Nations dealt with the issue of child welfare and slavery.

The 1930s was a much more challenging decade for the League of Nations. As economic depression spread across the world, countries put their own national interests above international co-operation. Sometimes this happened at the expense of another country's freedom or security: Japan invaded China, and Italy took Abyssinia. France and Great Britain used the veto rather than oppose the dictatorships that threatened the peace. The League of Nations looked increasingly weak.

There was further progress on humanitarian issues, such as action against slavery and people trafficking. Although developments made were minor, at least the issues were on the international agenda.

By the end of the 1930s war had already begun in Asia and Europe. The European empires dragged in Africa as well. The League of Nations had failed in its main purpose and, whatever else it might have achieved, this was what came to define it.

2.1. THE FAILURE OF THE LEAGUE OF NATIONS IN MANCHURIA AND ABYSSINIA

LEARNING OBJECTIVES

- Understand how the disputes in Manchuria (1931–33) and Abyssinia (1935–36) developed
- Evaluate the actions taken by the League of Nations in reaction to these disputes
- Explain the impact of the disputes in Manchuria and Abyssinia on the League of Nations.

1929 Wall Street Crash leads to global economic depression

January 1933 Hitler becomes chancellor of Germany
March 1933 Japan leaves the League of Nations
October 1933 Germany leaves the League of Nations

1936 Hitler remilitarises the Rhineland in breach of the Treaty of Versailles

September 1939 Germany invades Poland, beginning the Second World War
December 1939 The USSR is expelled from the League of Nations after attacking Finland

1931 Japan begins its takeover of Manchuria

September 1934 The USSR joins the League of Nations
December 1934 Wal-Wal Incident

1935 Italy invades Abyssinia

1937 Italy leaves the League of Nations

1938 Sudetenland Crisis

▲ Timeline of the 1930s

THE MANCHURIAN CRISIS, 1931–33

One of the most significant failures of the League of Nations was the Manchurian crisis.

In the 1920s Japan's army began losing confidence in its government, which at that time was supporting international disarmament initiatives. At the same time Japan was increasingly suffering economic difficulties. Then, in the 1930s, the Great Depression hit silk exports badly and industrial production also fell by 30 per cent. Japan was not resource-rich and this, combined with its growing population, contributed to falling standards of living, especially in 1930–32. The Japanese people therefore also became **disillusioned** with their government.

China offered a possible solution to Japan's problems. Politically it was weak, with many areas run by **warlords**. It also had large supplies of raw materials and could provide a vast market for Japanese exports. Manchuria was especially good for farming, and rich in coal and iron. Japan already controlled land around the Manchurian railway thanks to a 1905 Treaty.

In September 1931 a bomb exploded on the South Manchurian Railway. After the explosion, the Japanese army claimed it needed to restore order and took control of the town of Mukden.

China went to the League of Nations. By the time the issue was considered, in October, the Japanese army had also taken Chinchow, Manchuria's **administrative capital**. Japan then promised the League, and its fellow Council members, that it would withdraw as soon as it thought that the time right. It said that it had no ambitions in the area. Yet by January 1932, Japan had taken Shanghai. China again appealed to the League. In March 1932, Japan renamed Manchuria as Manchuko, which was to be an 'independent' state occupied by the Japanese army.

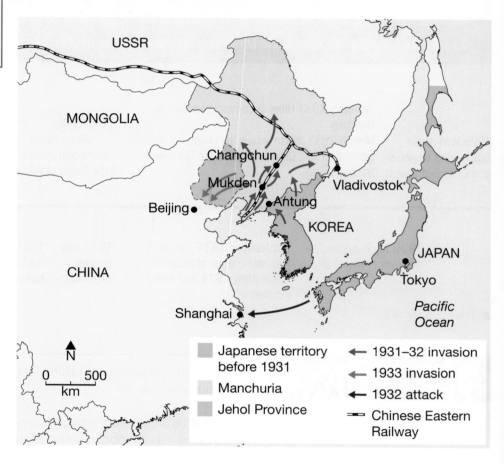

▶ Figure 2.1 The Manchurian Crisis, 1931–33

MANCHURIA: THE LEAGUE OF NATIONS' RESPONSE

The League of Nations responded to China's request by establishing the Lytton Commission to investigate the crisis in September 1931. The commission reported in September 1932 that the people of Manchuria did not want to become Manchuko, or to be governed by Japan. It advised that Manchuria become an **autonomous** Chinese state and that Japan should withdraw to the land it had been given in 1905.

In February 1933, the Assembly voted in favour of the Lytton Commission 42 votes to one. In March 1933, Japan left the League of Nations and kept control of Manchuko. In 1937 it launched a full-scale invasion of China. By this time, the Japanese army effectively controlled Japan's government and had established what was basically a military **dictatorship**.

KEY TERMS

autonomous self-governing; being able to make your own decisions

dictatorship a country that is ruled by one person who has complete power

WHY DID THE LEAGUE OF NATIONS NOT DO MORE IN SUPPORT OF MANCHURIA?

As a key member of the League of Nations with a permanent seat on the Council, Japan's promises that it had no ambitions in the region could not be ignored. Britain had strong reasons for wanting to believe them. It needed a good relationship with Japan because of its own interests in the Far East, and so was unwilling to challenge the Japanese. The British foreign secretary also told the British cabinet that Japan had reason to make complaints against China, even if the Japanese army had acted wrongly.

Many other western nations also had significant economic interests to protect, especially in Shanghai. Although the USA was not a member of the League, it did not want strong action against Japan. Doing nothing at all was not an option, however, because smaller countries (such as Finland) were demanding action.

THE IMPACT OF THE LEAGUE OF NATIONS' RESPONSE TO THE MANCHURIA CRISIS

KEY TERM

bilateral between two countries

The League of Nations' failure to deal effectively with Japan's aggression in China severely damaged its reputation. Increasingly in the 1930s, nations returned to traditional methods of **diplomacy** such as:
- **bilateral** treaties
- small alliances of carefully selected countries
- conference decisions based on national interests rather than international principles.

This was certainly the case when dealing with Hitler's Germany (see pages 34–35).

The Manchurian Crisis underlined key League of Nations weaknesses.
- Great powers seemed to be treated differently from smaller, less influential countries. Other events in the 1930s concerning Germany and Italy also confirmed this.
- The actions that the League of Nations could take did not deter aggressors; Japan simply left the League and suffered no sanctions as a result of its invasion of Manchuria.
- The League had no effective means of enforcing its decisions.
- The League's procedures took too long in comparison with the pace of events on the ground. It took 1 year for the Lytton Commission to issue its report, by which time the Japanese were well established in Manchuria.
- Even when its principles were defied, the League could not, or would not, apply its Covenant. This further weakened its international standing and importance.

SOURCE A

'The Doormat' by David Low, 1933.

ACTIVITY

1 Make a chart to explain why Japan took control of Manchuria. The chart should have columns headed: economic reasons; political reasons; other reasons.
2 To what extent was the League of Nations to blame for Japan's seizure of Manchuria? In pairs review the evidence and agree an answer. Put it on a value continuum (as shown). List your reasons underneath.

0% League of Nations' fault   100% League of Nations' fault

3 Compare your answer with another pair. Come up with a decision that everyone can agree with.

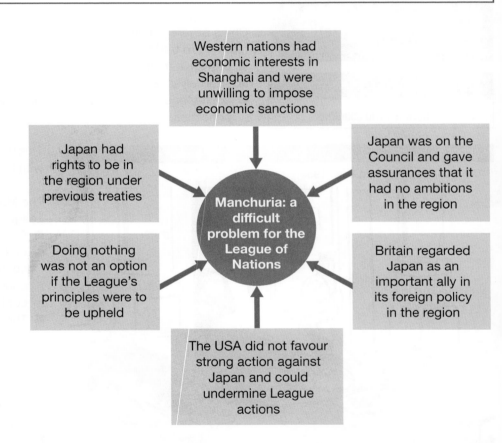

► **Figure 2.2** Manchuria: a difficult problem for the League of Nations

THE ABYSSINIAN CRISIS, 1935–36

Like Japan, Italy was a leading League of Nations member that wanted to expand. It already had colonies in Africa, but wanted to extend its hold on Italian Somaliland into Abyssinia. In 1930, the Italians had built a fort on the border between the two territories, at Wal-Wal. In 1932 Mussolini drew up plans to invade Abyssinia. Events in December 1934 gave him an excuse to do so. There as an incident at Wal-Wal resulting in the deaths of about 30 Italians and 90 Abyssinians. Mussolini demanded compensation for the Italian deaths. Abyssinia asked the League of Nations to step in.

The other great powers tried to influence Italy, but not through the League of Nations. This weakened the standing and relevance of the League further.

TIMELINE OF THE ABYSSINIA CRISIS

December 1934 Wal-Wal Incident; Abyssinia appeals to League of Nations for arbitration

March 1935 Abyssinia appeals to Council of League of Nations again

May 1935 Italy agrees to League of Nations arbitration of its dispute with Abyssinia

September 1935 The League of Nations finds neither side to blame for the Wal-Wal Incident

December 1935 Italy uses chemical weapons against Abyssinia

July 1936 Economic sanctions against Italy abandoned

December 1937 Italy withdraws from the League of Nations

January 1935 France holds talks with Italy, guaranteeing the Italians a strong presence in Africa; Italy continues preparing for war with Abyssinia. Abyssinian soldiers kill five Italians

April 1935 Great Britain, France and Italy meet at Stresa to discuss Germany

June 1935 Britain's Minister for League Affairs tries to appease Italy with parts of British Somaliland. Mussolini refuses and reminds Britain that France has guaranteed Italy a strong presence in Africa. He demands large chunks of Abyssinia

3 October 1935 Italian troops invade Abyssinia. The League's Council denounces war and prepares economic sanctions
10 October 1935 Majority decision in the League of Nations Assembly in favour of limited economic sanctions

May 1936 Addis Ababa, capital of Abyssinia, fell to the Italians. Mussolini declares himself emperor of Abyssinia. Abyssinia's leader, Haile Selassie, ends the war with Italy. Guatemala withdraws from the League of Nations due to the failure of collective security to protect Abyssinia

KEY TERM

balance of power a situation in which the political or military power of different countries is fairly equal – none is much more powerful than the others. Alternatively, if there are two larger nations of equal strength a small country can be said to 'hold the balance of power' because whichever of the two large countries it sides with will become the most powerful

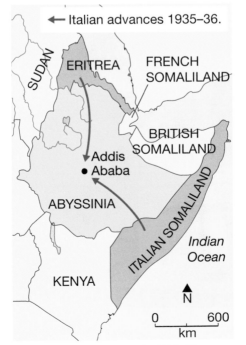

▲ **Figure 2.3** Abyssinia Crisis, 1935–36

SOURCE B

Extract from a report by the British government, June 1935. The report was known to Mussolini.

No vital interests exist in Abyssinia or in adjoining countries sufficient to oblige His Majesty's government to resist a conquest of Abyssinia by Italy.

France and Britain needed a good relationship with Italy to maintain a **balance of power** in Europe against Germany. Events in Europe were more important to them than the concerns of people thousands of kilometres away in Abyssinia. This can be seen in: France's negotiations with Italy in January 1935; the meeting at Stresa in April 1935; and Britain's dealings with Mussolini that June. Source B gives another reason why Italy was able to seize Abyssinia.

Although the League of Nations agreed economic sanctions against Italy, they were limited to:
- preventing sales of arms to Italy
- limiting credit to the Italian government and Italian firms
- an embargo on sales of oil to Italy.

Britain was not keen on the embargo in case it caused Italy to go to war in Europe. It was irrelevant anyway: the USA continued to supply oil to Italy, as did other non-League countries.

Ultimately Italy succeeded in taking Abyssinia, using chemical weapons and bombing raids by the Italian air force. Once Abyssinia had been taken over, economic sanctions against Italy stopped.

EXTEND YOUR KNOWLEDGE

The British and French foreign secretaries, Sir Samuel Hoare and Pierre Laval, drew up a plan to give Italy over 95,000 square km of Abyssinia. Hoare knew Mussolini from his time in the British intelligence service, which in 1917 had given Mussolini money to help fund his early days in Italian politics. When the Hoare-Laval plan became public there was shock and anger in Britain and France. Both men had to resign.

SOURCE C

Abyssinia's leader, Haile Selassie, addressing the League of Nations in July 1936, angry at how Abyssinia was let down by the League. Here he points out the wider consequences for the League, and what is at risk.

It is not merely a question of the settlement of Italian aggression. It is collective security: it is the very existence of the League of Nations. It is the confidence that each State is to place in international treaties. It is the value of promises made to small States that their integrity and their independence shall be respected and ensured.

EXTEND YOUR KNOWLEDGE

Rastafarianism is a religion based on the Bible. Rastafarians believe that the black race are the chosen people and that Haile Selassie is God. Selassie himself never believed this. The religion developed in the 1930s after Haile Selassie's coronation as emperor of Ethiopia. Its followers looked to him to lead Africans living in exile, due to slavery or escaping colonisation, back to their homeland.

France and Britain were imperial powers and their lack of action made it look like they were promoting imperialism

From Rome's point of view, the League had been weak, confused and irresolute

Abyssinia had been let down; this sent a poor message to smaller, weaker nations

Consequences of the Abyssinian Crisis

After Abyssinia, collective security was increasingly side-lined

The League had imposed half-hearted and ineffective sanctions

The great powers had again used diplomacy outside the League; the League played very little part in the drift to war 1938–39

▲ **Figure 2.4** The consequences of Abyssinia for the League of Nations

SOURCE D

Abyssinia's leader, Emperor Haile Selassie, addresses the League of Nations in 1936.

ACTIVITY

1 Develop Haile Selassie's speech in Source C. What might he say next to reinforce his points?

2 Review the outcomes of the territorial disputes dealt with by the League of Nations in the 1920s. Compare them with the outcomes in the 1930s. What do you notice about the League's achievements? How can you explain these differences? You might like to discuss this in pairs before writing up your answer.

EXAM-STYLE QUESTION

A01   **A02**

Explain **two** ways in which the response of the League of Nations to the Manchurian Crisis of 1931–33 was similar to its response to the Greek–Bulgarian War of 1925.   **(6 marks)**

HINT

For 6 marks you need to give two specific similarities.

2.2 THE ROLE OF THE GREAT POWERS IN THE 1930S: THE LEAGUE OF NATIONS' VETO

LEARNING OBJECTIVES

- Understand why the great powers were important to the League of Nations
- Evaluate the use of the veto in the League of Nations
- Understand how membership issues affected the League of Nations.

The great powers of the 1930s inside the League of Nations were:
- France and Great Britain
- Germany and Italy until they left in 1933 and 1937
- The USSR from 1934 until it too left in 1939.

The greatest world power was the USA, but it was not a member of the League.

These countries were great powers because of their economies, developing technology and (in the case of Britain and France) empires that stretched throughout Africa and Asia.

As the world's most powerful countries, the great powers were needed to play a leading role in international relations. This was especially true in the League of Nations' Council, which was where its key decisions were made. The Council met 107 times between 1920 and 1939 and, when it worked effectively, it showed that international co-operation was possible.

As the wealthiest country of all, the USA's refusal to join the League of Nations weakened it considerably. Germany was allowed to join in 1926 although it could not vote on matters concerning the **implementation** of the Treaty of Versailles. By the time the USSR joined in 1934, Germany and Japan had left the League, as did Italy in 1937.

Membership problems were not the only reason why the League was often too weak to enforce its principles and decisions. In the cases of Germany, Japan and Italy the League was faced with **dictators** who simply ignored it. There was nothing the League could do: without armed forces of its own, the League could not stop Germany, Japan and Italy taking land from other countries; and the Great Depression meant that other nations did not want to use economic sanctions as a punishment.

THE PROBLEM OF THE LEAGUE OF NATIONS' VETO

The Council voted on how to deal with disputes, and the Assembly (if it were meeting) voted on decisions taken by the Council. All votes had to be unanimous. So, although there was no actual power of **veto** in the League, it is often talked about because by voting against something, a member could effectively veto it.

There were also some decisions that required only a majority vote, including:
- electing the temporary members of the Council
- admission of new members to the League
- issues resulting from the post-World War I peace treaties that concerned the armaments of the defeated powers.

SOURCE E

From *The Origin, Structure and Working of the League of Nations*, a book on the League of Nations published in 1929.

Critics often lose sight of the fact that the League is an association of independent states and so must proceed by way of unanimous compromise and not by majorities imposing decisions upon minorities. No state today will … spend money or take action … because of a vote of foreign powers … any settlement must be agreed to by all parties and not imposed on some by the rest.

As Source E points out, it was important that all members of the League of Nations agreed to its decisions unanimously. This meant that no nation had to take action that was against its own interests. However, this also meant that one nation could veto something agreed upon by every other member state if it was not in its own interests. This could lead to national interests being put above international ones.

2.3 THE ROLE OF THE GREAT POWERS IN THE 1930S: THE FAILURE TO CURB THE DICTATORS

LEARNING OBJECTIVES

- Understand why dictatorships developed between the First World War and the Second World War
- Explain why the League of Nations could not resist aggressive dictators
- Understand why the League of Nations appeared irrelevant in the 1930s.

THE CHANGING POLITICAL LANDSCAPE

KEY TERM

fascist someone who believes in strong central government, state control of major industries, aggressive nationalism, the cruel suppression of opposition and a powerful military

Political extremism often accompanies economic hardship. As economies struggled after the Wall Street Crash of 1929, people looked for strong leadership and fast solutions to their problems. In the 1930s, dictatorships took power in many countries, and across Central and Southern America there were military coups, for example, in Guatemala and Peru. Dictatorships also took power in Europe and Asia and in several key League of Nations member states, including some of the great powers. Italy was already run by a fascist dictator, Benito Mussolini, who had come to power in the 1920s. In both Japan and Germany, however, dictatorships came to power after the Wall Street Crash.

DICTATOR	COUNTRY	POLITICS	TERRITORIES TAKEN
Benito Mussolini 1922–45	Italy	Fascism	Abyssinia 1935–36
Emperor Hirohito and the Japanese Military 1926–45	Japan	Imperialism, nationalism	Manchuria 1931–33 Full-scale attack on China 1937
Adolf Hitler 1933–45	Germany	Nazism	Sudetenland 1938 Czechoslovakia 1939 Anschluss with Austria 1938

Japan, Germany and Italy all developed aggressive foreign policies to deal with their economic difficulties. These involved invading other territories to exploit their resources and markets. As a result, international tensions increased. Unfortunately, the League failed to protect the countries that were victims of the invasions. The **economic depression** of the 1930s made governments focus much more strongly on national interests. Solving their own economic problems became far more important than international politics. The League's strongest weapon, economic sanctions, damaged the nations imposing them as well as punishing the aggressors. Economic sanctions therefore made much less sense in the 1930s, especially as Germany and Japan were both important trading nations.

League membership was an important weakness when it came to issues concerning peace, disarmament and curbing the dictators. The USA was not a member, nor was the USSR until 1934 – by which time Germany and Japan had left. The great powers' involvement would be essential if disarmament were to work and peace be maintained. Treaties on these issues were therefore often made outside of the League of Nations. As a result, the League appeared irrelevant to the main reason it was created.

> **KEY TERM**
>
> economic depression a sustained period of the slowing down of economic activity, i.e. producing goods and buying or selling them

EXTEND YOUR KNOWLEDGE

Benito Mussolini, dictator of Italy 1922–45, is generally considered to be the founder of fascism. He had three key beliefs. Firstly, the nation must come first and should be ruled by a government that has the power to control everything. This requires a dictatorship. Secondly, the nation should expand and grow stronger. Ultimately it should aim to rule the world. This means that it needs an aggressive foreign policy and a large military. Thirdly, anyone who does not conform with the government is wrong and must be punished, even executed. This means that an independent police force or legal system cannot be allowed and that education and information must be controlled. Other political parties are banned.

Hitler developed his own form of fascism, Nazism. In Nazi Germany, the nation was defined racially and other 'inferior' races were persecuted.

DISARMAMENT

Disarmament was part of the League's covenant, although exactly what that meant was a little unclear, as Source F shows.

SOURCE F

From the covenant of the League of Nations.

The Members of the League recognise that the maintenance of peace requires the reduction of national armaments to the lowest point [necessary for] national safety and the enforcement by common action of international obligations.

The Council, taking account of the geographical situation and circumstances of each State, shall formulate plans for such reduction for the consideration and action of the several Governments.

From the start, a basic problem for the League of Nations was that the leading powers all believed that being better armed than their rivals was the best deterrent to being attacked. Therefore, although it was frequently discussed at Council and Assembly meetings, very little progress towards disarmament was made. There was, however, some progress outside the League.

THE WORLD DISARMAMENT CONFERENCE 1932–34

Between 1932 and 1934 there was a World Disarmament Conference. It included the USA and the USSR along with other non-League countries.

A great deal changed immediately before and during the conference that impacted upon the decisions made.
- In September 1931, Japan attacked Manchuria and in January 1932 it took Shanghai.
- In January 1933, Hitler became Chancellor of Germany.
- In March 1933, Japan left the League of Nations.
- In October 1933, Germany also left the League of Nations.

Once Germany and Japan left the League and began following more aggressive foreign policies, other countries were far less willing to go ahead with disarmament. Furthermore, there was a range of technical difficulties. One major difficulty was deciding which weapons were **defensive** and which were offensive.

The failure of the 1932 World Disarmament Conference to agree on anything by 1934, together with Japan and Germany leaving the League of Nations, damaged the League's reputation considerably. Indeed, as the 1930s wore on the League of Nations became increasingly irrelevant in international relations.

▼ Who proposed what at the World Disarmament Conference, 1932–34

COUNTRY	DEMANDS	COUNTRY	DEMANDS
France	Proposed that the League of Nations should control the world's most powerful weapons and have an independent police force	UK	Suggested getting rid of all offensive weapons – but how was an offensive weapon different from a defensive one?
Germany	Demanded equality with states that had not had their military cut, like Germany had under the Treaty of Versailles	USSR	Advocated the abolition of all weapons. The USSR was still industrially and technologically a long way behind the other major powers in 1932

WHY WAS THE LEAGUE OF NATIONS INCREASINGLY IRRELEVANT IN THE 1930S?

Developments after 1929 led to collective security becoming less likely. Nations returned to traditional patterns of diplomacy, such as bilateral treaties and small conferences that focused more on regional needs. This was especially true in Europe, where Hitler was challenging the Treaty of Versailles and western European nations felt threatened by the USSR. Once dictators like Hitler began their aggressive foreign policies, disarmament was no longer an option for many League members. From the mid 1930s, Britain and France too began re-arming as the prospect of war seemed more probable

ACTIVITY

1 Write up a list of ways in which the great powers weakened the League of Nations.
2 Working in pairs, produce a poster, newspaper editorial or speech promoting the League of Nations in the early 1930s. Why is its role even more important now than in the 1920s?

FAILURE TO CURB THE DICTATORS: HITLER AND GERMANY

Once Hitler came to power, it wasn't long before he took Germany out of the League of Nations. He then began rearming and expanding in direct **contravention** of the Treaty of Versailles.

▼ Hitler's violations of the Treaty of Versailles

▼ TREATY OF VERSAILLES TERMS	▼ HITLER'S ACTIONS
The Covenant of the League of Nations was the first item of the Treaty of Versailles. Germany had therefore signed up to the League's covenant	Germany left the League of Nations in October 1933. Hitler went on to expand Germany beyond the territorial boundaries allowed under the Treaty of Versailles – which was also in direct contravention of the League's covenant.
No German air force; no submarines; no tanks; limited navy; army of 100,000 men only; conscription banned	Hitler rearmed Germany. In 1935 he announced that Germany had the Luftwaffe (military air force) and reintroduced conscription. In 1935 Hitler and Britain signed the Anglo-German Naval Treaty. Its terms allowed Germany to have a navy as long as it wasn't greater than Britain's.
The Rhineland **demilitarised**	In 1936, Hitler remilitarised the Rhineland.
Annexation of Austria (Anschluss) forbidden	In 1938, Austria was unified with Germany. The tanks that drove into Vienna also showed how German military strength was growing in contravention of the Treaty of Versailles.
Germany's borders redrawn to contribute to the creation of Czechoslovakia	In 1938, Hitler demanded the Sudetenland, part of Germany that had been given to Czechoslovakia in the Treaty of Versailles. Britain, France and Italy agreed to his demands at the Munich Conference. Hitler took the rest of Czechoslovakia in 1939.

KEY TERM

annexation absorbing one territory into another; Anschluss refers to the annexation of Austria by Germany

▶ **Figure 2.5** Germany's expansion into Austria and Czechoslovakia, 1938–39

WHY DIDN'T THE LEAGUE OF NATIONS STOP HITLER?

By the 1930s, attitudes towards Germany were softening. It had been especially badly hit by the economic depression following the Wall Street Crash and there was a growing feeling that the Treaty of Versailles had been too harsh. Fear of the USSR remained strong, however, and a well-armed Germany could act as a buffer to prevent communism spreading into western Europe.

Furthermore, Germany left the League of Nations in October 1933, so diplomacy to appease Hitler was conducted outside of the League. For example, Great Britain even supported Hitler's breaking of the Treaty of Versailles with the Anglo–German Naval Treaty in 1935 (see table on page 34).

In 1938 Hitler claimed that the Sudetenland ought to be part of Germany. The Sudetenland formed part of the German / Czechoslovakian border. Britain, France and Italy negotiated directly with Germany, bypassing the League of Nations altogether. They appeased Hitler by giving him what he wanted. By spring 1939 all of Czechoslovakia was under German control. He had taken it unopposed.

There was little that the League of Nations could do to prevent Hitler acting as he pleased, especially if Britain and France appeased him. As far as curbing Germany was concerned, the League was proving to be irrelevant – including to the great powers that had permanent seats on the Council.

ACTIVITY

1 Who is climbing out of the baby's cot in the cartoon? Why do you think he is shown with a knife?
2 Who do the angels in the cartoon represent? What is their attitude to the baby?
3 What event(s) do you think the cartoonist is representing? Look at the date to help you.
4 Work in pairs. Do you think that the fact the cartoon is from the USSR is important? Why? Discuss your answer and be prepared to feed back to the class.
5 How accurate do you think this cartoon is about events in the 1930s? Explain your answer with reference to what you have learned so far.

SOURCE G

A Soviet cartoon of 1936 showing western nations as Hitler's protectors.

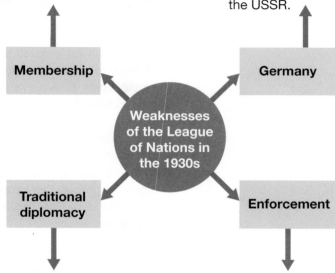

- The USA was large enough to have economic and political influence, but was not a member.
- Japan, Germany and Italy left when they broke League principles.

- Attitudes to Germany had softened since Versailles and Wall Street Crash.
- A strong, armed Germany would be a buffer against the USSR.

Membership

Germany

Weaknesses of the League of Nations in the 1930s

Traditional diplomacy

Enforcement

- National interests often remained more important than international ones.
- Much diplomacy was conducted outside the League, for example, Britain and France with Italy and Germany.

- The League had no military or police force of its own.
- Countries were unwilling to impose economic sanctions after the Wall Street Crash.

▶ **Figure 2.6** Why was the League of Nations weak in the 1930s?

EXAM-STYLE QUESTION

Explain **two** causes of the League of Nations' failure to stop Hitler.   **(8 marks)**

A01   **A02**

SKILL   ADAPTIVE LEARNING

HINT

Do not confuse causes with examples. Think about the causes first, and then identify examples to help you develop your explanation.

2.4 THE WORK OF THE SPECIALISED AGENCIES

LEARNING OBJECTIVES

☐ Describe the work of the League's Child Welfare Committee and the Slavery Commission

☐ Evaluate the impact of the League's Child Welfare Committee and the Slavery Commission

☐ Understand how the League of Nations came to an end.

THE CHILD WELFARE COMMITTEE

Children can face poverty and hardship in all nations, even those with the most developed economies (see Source H). Whenever adults suffer, children often suffer more.

Child welfare was an especially urgent issue in the 1920s and 1930s because the First World War led to huge numbers of refugees and orphans. Improving child welfare was also an important long-term strategy aimed at ensuring peace. It was thought that well-educated, -fed and -cared for children would be less likely to turn to political extremism, crime and violence as they grew. The League of Nations believed that if it worked to ensure children were well looked after, they in turn would support the League as adults.

SOURCE H

Child poverty in Paris, France – one of the great powers – in 1931.

SOURCE I

From the 1924 Geneva Declaration of the Rights of the Child.

The child that is hungry must be fed; the child that is sick must be nursed; the child that is backward must be helped; the delinquent child must be reclaimed; and the orphan and the waif must be sheltered and succoured.

There were several League of Nations' commissions whose work involved children's issues that crossed international borders, including health, slavery, refugees and the ILO (International Labour Organization). There were also other, non-League groups and charities, such as the International Save the Children Fund (ISCF). The Child Welfare Committee (CWC) acted as an umbrella organisation for these other commissions and organisations. It also researched and discussed issues concerning children.

WHAT DID THE CWC ACHIEVE?

Many countries saw child welfare as a national issue and resented or ignored the CWC's recommendations. Sex education and contraception are two good examples of areas many considered unsuitable for League intervention. Other topics dealt with in early sessions of the CWC included: state benefits for families; physical activity; the rights of illegitimate children; and children with disabilities.

During the 1930s, the CWC increasingly reported on social problems affecting children, mainly homelessness and poverty, because of global economic depression. It collected, analysed and published good quality data. Its findings proved strong links between living conditions, wages and the basic standards of nutrition children required.

The CWC also looked into juvenile crime (crime committed by young people). It believed that the answer to the problem was measures preventing children from turning to crime in the first place rather than punishing them for crimes after they had been committed.

Although its impact was not great, the CWC established approaches to the welfare of children that would make an important contribution to the work later done by UNICEF. And, even though the countries that signed it did not always keep it to, the Geneva Declaration of the Rights of the Child clearly stated that children had different needs to adults and that these must be satisfied and protected. Acceptance of this was a good first step for future initiatives because it recognised that all children everywhere needed certain basic rights and opportunities.

THE LEAGUE OF NATIONS: SLAVERY

The League of Nations was determined to tackle the problem of slavery on an international scale. In 1926 it established the Convention on Slavery, Servitude, Forced Labour and Similar Institutions. This defined slavery and identified other ways of trading in slaves including:

■ enslavement as payment for a debt
■ 'adopting' children who were, in fact, being enslaved
■ selling a child and calling the payment a dowry.

The League of Nations proposed that the best way to deal with slavery was to outlaw it in every country. It made other proposals including:

■ the transport of slaves at sea was to be considered an act of piracy
■ European and Egyptian ships were to be allowed to pursue slave ships into countries' own territorial waters.

In 1930 the International Labour Organization (ILO) defined forced labour as 'all work or service which is exacted from any person under the menace of any penalty' rather than being offered voluntarily.

By 1929, the Convention had been ratified by 30 governments. It made positive progress in dealing with slavery, encouraging its end in Nepal (1926), Burma (1928), and Jordan and Persia (1929). In 1929 the League found considerable evidence of slavery in Liberia. In 1930, the Liberian government asked the League to investigate slavery and forced labour in Liberia, which led to reforms abolishing slavery there.

In 1931 the League reported slavery was continuing in some lands bordering the Red Sea, where slaves were being transported from Abyssinia and the Somali coasts. Liberia asked the League to help it make the necessary reforms to end slavery. The League also made the abolition (end) of slavery a precondition of Arab nations joining it.

Although slavery was not ended, the League of Nations took important steps to making it unacceptable across the world. The League's Mandates Commission also worked against slavery.

THE LEAGUE OF NATIONS: PEOPLE TRAFFICKING

People trafficking was different from slavery, although those who were trafficked often ended up in similar circumstances. One particular problem was the forced trafficking of women and children for prostitution. In 1921 the League held an international conference that led to an agreement called the Convention for the Suppression of the Traffic in Women and Children. This protected girls and younger women by raising the age at which women could agree to being trafficked to 21.

From 1924 to 1926, the League investigated people trafficking in Europe, the Mediterranean and America. In 1929 it investigated the Near, Middle and Far East. It found hundreds of girls, most aged between 14 and 16, being trafficked into prostitution – sometimes even by their own parents.

The League's intervention in the trafficking of women and children achieved three important things.
1   It highlighted forced prostitution, and the trade in prostitutes, as a global issue. Until then, trying to tackle the problem had been the work of national, often voluntary groups.
2   Rather than seeing the prostitutes as being the guilty parties, or blaming them for their situation, it began to look at the problem differently. It looked at the supply of, and demand for, people trafficking. In 1927 it issued a report upon how the trade actually worked by gathering detailed information from both prostitutes and traffickers.
3   In 1937, the Conference of Central Authorities of Eastern Countries was held in Java. It succeeded in getting several of the nations attending to agree to raise the age of marriage and the age of consent, as well as abolish legal brothels (places where prostitutes work).

It is not easy to measure the impact of the League's work on trafficking in women and children as there were no obvious, major improvements. Not all those who signed the Convention made trafficking a crime. The Convention itself did nothing to protect women who agreed to be prostitutes, nor people trafficked within their own country; and it did not make owning a brothel illegal – these all remained domestic matters for individual nations.

ACTIVITY

1   Draw up two lists of outcomes, one for the League of Nations' work on child welfare, one for its work on slavery and people trafficking. Which do you think was more successful and why?
2   Design a web-page or wall display to inform people of the work done by the League of Nations on social and humanitarian issues. Pick at least one commission from chapters one and two. You could do this in small groups or pairs.

EXAM-STYLE QUESTION

A01 **A02**

SKILLS ▸ PROBLEM SOLVING, REASONING, DECISION MAKING

How far did the League of Nations' ability to fulfil its aims change between 1920 and 1939?

You may use the following in your answer:
- the League of Nations' handling of territorial crises
- the League of Nations' humanitarian work.

You **must** also use information of your own.   **(16 marks)**

HINT

Be clear about the League of Nations' key aim(s). The question focuses on the change in the League of Nations' effectiveness in delivering them. What were the main changes or turning points in this timeframe?

THE END OF THE LEAGUE OF NATIONS

The League's last act was to expel the USSR after it invaded Finland. After that, the only 1930s great powers still in the League were France and Britain.

The League of Nations played no role in the Second World War. It was, after all, based on international co-operation. It was not designed to operate during such a large-scale conflict. Its last Secretary-General, Seán Lester, remained in Geneva during the war. His role was to ensure that the League survived until it could be legally ended. Some agencies, such as the ILO and the Mandates Commission, also continued to exist but could not do much.

The League of Nations ceased to exist in 1946. By this time its successor, the United Nations (UN), had already been founded. Some of the League's work, such as its work with children, refugees, health, the ILO, and the Mandates Commission, was transferred to the UN, where it was built upon.

CONCLUSION

The League of Nations failed in its most important aim: maintaining international peace. The weaknesses that had been problems from its creation became very clear in the 1930s. This was largely because of the Great Depression and changing international circumstances. In 1937, Japan launched a full-scale invasion of China; in 1939 Germany invaded Poland and the world was at war only 21 years after the First World War had ended.

RECAP

RECALL QUIZ

1. In what years did Germany and the USSR join the League of Nations?
2. Name two countries that became dictatorships in the 1930s.
3. Name one disarmament initiative made by the League of Nations.
4. When did Japan, Germany and Italy leave the League of Nations?
5. Who signed a naval treaty in 1935?
6. What was the name given to Manchuria by Japan?
7. When did Abyssinia appeal to the League of Nations over Italy's behaviour?
8. Give two economic sanctions the League of Nations agreed to against Italy.
9. What did the Geneva Declaration of 1924 concern?
10. Give two countries where slavery was abolished in the 1920s.

CHECKPOINT

STRENGTHEN
S1 What does the word 'veto' mean?
S2 Give two ways in which Germany broke the Treaty of Versailles.
S3 Give one thing achieved by the CWC and one thing achieved by the slavery commission.

CHALLENGE
C1 Give two problems that the League of Nations had to deal with because of the Wall Street Crash.
C2 Give two reasons why Italy was able to take control of Abyssinia.
C3 Describe two successful humanitarian initiatives carried out by the League of Nations in the 1930s.

SUMMARY

- The Wall Street Crash made it much harder for the League of Nations to fulfil its aims.
- The great powers were especially ineffective in dealing with dictators.
- Japan, Germany and Italy all left the League and conducted aggressive foreign policies during the 1930s.
- Disarmament made little progress and what was achieved was done outside the League.
- Britain and France were more focused on Germany than wider international issues.
- The USA not being a member of the League continued to hamper its effectiveness.
- Manchuria and Abyssinia were key tests and turning points for the League of Nations.
- The League of Nations continued its humanitarian work throughout the 1930s.
- The League's work against slavery made some strong progress but its work supporting children less so, although a great deal of useful research was done.

EXAM GUIDANCE: PART (B) QUESTIONS

A01 **A02**

SKILL ADAPTIVE LEARNING

Question to be answered: Explain two causes of the League of Nations' failure to deal effectively with the Manchurian Crisis of 1931–33. (8 marks)

1 **Analysis Question 1: What is the question type testing?**
In this question you have to demonstrate that you have knowledge and understanding of the key features and characteristics of the period studied. In this particular case it is knowledge and understanding of the League of Nations' involvement in the Manchurian Crisis of 1931–33.

You also have to explain, analyse and make judgements about historical events and periods to explain why something happened.

2 **Analysis Question 2: What do I have to do to answer the question well?**
Obviously you have to write about the League of Nations' handling of the Manchurian Crisis. But it isn't just a case of writing everything you know. You have to write about why it failed. To do this well, you need to give detail showing what the League tried to do, but you also need to make sure you are explaining why those efforts led to failure. We call this explaining why your chosen causes produced the given outcome (i.e. the League's failure in Manchuria).

In this case, there are several causes of the League's failures. You might write about the League's lack of armed forces to support its decisions or how the national interests of Council members were more important than events in Manchuria, for example.

3 **Analysis Question 3: Are there any techniques I can use to make it very clear that I am doing what is needed to be successful?**
This is an 8-mark question and you need to make sure you leave enough time to answer the other two questions fully (they are worth 22 marks in total). Therefore you need to get straight in to writing your answer. The question asks for two causes, so it's a good idea to write two paragraphs and to begin each paragraph with phrases like 'One cause was…', 'Another cause was…'. You will get a maximum of 4 marks for each cause you explain, so make sure you give two causes.

How many marks you score for each cause will depend on how well you use accurate and factual information to explain why the clashes occurred.

Answer A

There were two reasons why the League of Nations failed in Manchuria. One is that other nations did not want to take strong action against Japan and the other is that the League was not strong enough to enforce any decisions it did make.

What are the strengths and weaknesses of Answer A?

It isn't a very good answer. It does give two reasons, as the question asks, but it hasn't provided factual information to support those reasons, or explained why the League failed. It is doubtful that this answer would score more than two marks.

Answer B

There were two reasons why the League of Nations failed in Manchuria.

The first reason was that other nations did not want to take strong action against Japan that would damage their own national interests. The Great Depression was causing problems across the world and so a measure such as economic sanctions would make existing economic problems worse. Furthermore, Britain, one of the permanent members of the Council, did not want to lose Japan's support in the Far East as it had its own interests there. The British foreign minister had even said that Japan had reason to complain about China even if its army had acted wrongly. So national interests meant some nations were not prepared to take the actions necessary to deal with the crisis effectively.

Another reason why the League of Nations failed in Manchuria was because it was unable to enforce its decisions when up against a powerful country like Japan. When the Lytton Commission reported in 1933, declaring that Manchuria ought to be an independent Chinese state, Japan simply withdrew from the League of Nations and continued to occupy 'Manchuko'. There was nothing that the League could do. Not only did the League have no armed forces with which to protect member nations against aggressors such as Japan, but without the USA being a member, trading sanctions did not have much of an impact. The USA was the world's largest economy and the most important trading nation for many countries – and was also another country that did not want to take strong action against Japan because of their own national interests. This meant that any economic sanctions imposed by the League could be undermined by the Americans, who were not part of the League at this time. So lack of power meant Japan was allowed to 'get away with' its invasion of Manchuria.

What are the strengths and weaknesses of Answer B?

This is an excellent answer. It gives two causes and provides factual support in showing how those causes brought about the clashes. The answer uses information such as the USA not being a member without getting distracted by explaining why it wasn't – the question was not testing knowledge and understanding of that issue. It would be likely to receive full marks.

Challenge a friend

Use the Student Book to set a part (b) question for a friend. Then look at the answer. Does it do the following things?

☐ Provide two causes
☐ Provide detailed information to support the causes
☐ Show how the causes led to the given outcome.

If it does, you can tell your friend that the answer is very good!

3. SETTING UP THE UNITED NATIONS ORGANISATION AND ITS WORK TO 1964

LEARNING OBJECTIVES

- Understand the structure of the United Nations
- Understand the structural problems of the United Nations
- Evaluate the performance of the United Nations in Palestine, Korea and the Congo.

As with the League of Nations, the concept of the United Nations was developed during wartime. The League of Nations provided a model (although a far from perfect one) to follow. Those who designed the structure of the United Nations aimed to avoid the key mistakes made by the League.

What they were unable to control, however, was the way international relations developed after the Second World War. This was to have a huge impact on the new organisation's effectiveness. One key weakness of the League of Nations had been the lack of its own armed forces to enforce its decisions. Although there were plans for such a force for the new United Nations, they were never realised. The Cold War made any military co-operation between the world's major powers impossible. It also weakened international co-operation on other fronts, including in key trouble spots such as the Middle East and Sub-Saharan Africa.

3.1 SETTING UP THE UN AND ITS STRUCTURE

LEARNING OBJECTIVES

- Understand the roles of the key parts of the UN
- Explain the problems with the structure of the UN
- Understand key UN social, economic and humanitarian work.

THE SETTING UP OF THE UN

1941 Roosevelt and Churchill met and agreed the foundations of the United Nations

1945 The United Nations Organisation is founded in San Francisco

1943 Moscow Declaration by the USA, USSR, China and Great Britain recognised the need for an international body to replace the League of Nations

In August 1941 US President Franklin D. Roosevelt and British Prime Minister Winston Churchill met to discuss their war aims. These included an international organisation founded on the principles of freedom, self-determination, free trade and improved standards of living.

When the UN was officially founded in San Francisco in June 1945, 50 nations signed its charter. More nations followed in the years immediately after the war. The powers defeated in the war did not join until 1955 (Italy); 1956 (Japan); and 1973 (West Germany and East Germany).

EXTEND YOUR KNOWLEDGE

After the war Germany was divided into four zones. These zones developed into two different countries: West Germany and East Germany. After the Second World War, the USSR and the USA became involved in a Cold War (a war of words and propaganda, rather than military hostilities). During the Cold War, West Germany sided with the USA, but East Germany was an ally of the USSR.

THE UNITED NATIONS' CHARTER AND ITS KEY PRINCIPLES

The key aims of the UN, as reflected in its charter, are to:
- prevent war and maintain international peace and security
- promote human rights
- solve problems through international law and co-operation
- promote a better quality of life for all peoples.

President Truman addresses delegates at the signing of the UN Charter.

THE STRUCTURE OF THE UN

The structure of the UN is similar to that of its predecessor, the League of Nations. There is a General Assembly made up of all member states and a Security Council, consisting of permanent members and temporary ones, which acts as its **executive**. There is a Secretariat administering and implementing the policies decided upon by the General Assembly and Security Council, and there are a number of bodies and agencies tackling social, economic and humanitarian projects.

THE SECRETARY-GENERAL

The Secretary-General is the public face of the UN and is elected every 5 years. The most important part of the Secretary-General's job is trying to solve international disputes and bringing threats to world peace to the attention of the Security Council. In carrying out this role the Secretary deals with national governments and other representatives from the member states, as well as the General Assembly and the Economic and Social Council. It is vital that the Secretary-General is independent and above national politics. Despite having such a high profile, the Secretary's powers are limited, as UN decisions are made in the Security Council.

Trygve Lie
Norway
1946–52

Dag Hammarskjöld
Sweden
1953–61

U Thant
Myanmar
1961–71

Kurt Waldheim
Austria
1972–81

Javier Pérez de Cuéllar
Peru
1982–91

Boutros Boutros-Ghali
Egypt
1992–96

Kofi Annan
Ghana
1997–2006

Ban Ki-Moon
South Korea
2007–16

▲ Figure 3.1 Secretaries-General of the United Nations 1945–2016

THE ECONOMIC AND SOCIAL COUNCIL

The Economic and Social Council is central to supporting countries to develop according to the UN's internationally agreed goals. It has 54 members, each elected for 3-year terms, who oversee **sustainable development**, human rights and the UN's five regional development commissions. The Economic and Social Council is seen as vital to the UN's mission because economic depression was one of the key causes of the Second World War.

THE TRUSTEESHIP COUNCIL (MANDATES COMMISSION)

The Trusteeship Council was very active after the Second World War as the old European empires collapsed. Its role was similar to the League of Nations' Mandates Commission. It oversaw countries on the path to independence. It has not been used since Palau gained independence in 1994, and only meets as necessary.

THE INTERNATIONAL COURT OF JUSTICE

The International Court of Justice (ICJ) sits at The Hague, like the PICJ that it replaced. Its 15 judges are elected for 9-year terms by the General Assembly and Security Council. It oversees disputes between nations according to international law. It also advises the UN and its agencies and commissions on a range of issues. Given that the UN is dedicated to maintaining international peace, the ICJ plays an important role. Once a country agrees to take a case to the ICJ it must accept its decision.

KEY TERM

sustainable development improving economic growth and standards of living in a way which does not use up the earth's resources

▼ An overview of the key bodies of the United Nations

General Assembly	All UN members sit in the General Assembly. It meets annually, or more often if necessary. It elects non-permanent members of the Security Council; votes for ICJ judges; and appoints the Secretary-General based on the Security Council's recommendations. It debates and makes recommendations on a wide range of issues. Each country has one vote. Recommendations on peace and security need a two-thirds majority to pass.
Security Council	Fifteen countries sit on the Security Council, five are permanent: China, France, Great Britain, Russia and the USA. Non-permanent members are elected for 2-year terms and there are three from Africa; two from Western Europe and Oceania, Asia, Latin America; and one from Eastern Europe. The Security Council has the primary responsibility for maintaining international peace and security. It also votes for ICJ judges. The Security Council enforces sanctions and authorises the use of force to maintain or restore international peace and security. Any executive decisions can be passed by a simple majority, but must include all five permanent members. This means permanent members have right of veto. Decisions are binding on UN members.
Economic and Social Council	Has 54 members elected for 3-year terms. It is central to the UN's system for developing and implementing social, economic and environmental policies. It oversees and monitors the UN's five regional development commissions, sustainable development and human rights. It co-ordinates, reviews and makes recommendations based on the work of other UN bodies.
Secretariat	It carries out the day-to-day work of the UN. Led by the Secretary-General it puts the UN's decisions into action. It has offices around the world. Sixteen thousand employees and volunteers work to put UN programmes and policies into action.
International Court of Justice	The ICJ sits at The Hague. Its 15 judges are elected for 9-year terms. It settles disputes between nations brought to the UN according to international law. It also advises on legal questions raised by the UN, its commissions and specialised agencies. If a country agrees to its case going to the ICJ, it must accept its decision.
Trusteeship Council	It was created to oversee the process of decolonisation after the Second World War, helping colonies to become independent states. Its importance has declined as most territories in the world have become self-governing, independent states.

SOURCE B

UN Security Council in session.

KEY TERMS

subsidiary body an additional or supplementary part of a main body or organisation

resolution a formal decision or statement agreed on by a group of people, especially after a vote

superpower a nation that has very great military and political power

ACTIVITY

1 Identify similarities and differences in the set-up of the United Nations and the League of Nations.
2 In pairs, decide which difference was the most important improvement. Explain your choice.
3 In groups of four, look at the list of principles of the UN on page 45. Which key bodies of the UN would have a role in fulfilling those principles?

OVERVIEW OF THE UNITED NATIONS

The diagram on page 50 shows the key parts of the UN. There are dozens of **subsidiary bodies**, which mainly focus on humanitarian, social and economic issues. Some deal with long-term development programmes; others react to crises as they develop, providing short-term aid and support. The diagram shows how large a structure the United Nations has become. It is not necessary to know all of the UN's different parts, but the diagram does illustrate some key points.

- The Secretary-General is the public face of the UN, working directly with governments around the world as well as the principal bodies that make up the United Nations. The Secretary-General is therefore very influential, but the power to make and enforce decisions lies with the Security Council.
- The General Assembly and the Social and Economic Council are at the heart of the organisation. They work with each other as well as with the Security Council, the World Trade Organization (WTO) and a variety of UN agencies.

Much of the diagram concerns humanitarian work as well as social and economic development programmes. This is because that is where most of the UN's day-to-day work is focused.

The ICJ is set apart, as any state can submit a dispute to it without going through the UN.

ACTIVITY

Produce a poster, leaflet or write a newspaper article persuading people of the benefits of the new United Nations and encouraging them to support it. You should refer to key details about its structure, aims and what impact it should have on the lives of ordinary people.

STRUCTURAL PROBLEMS OF THE UN

The UN aimed to avoid the League of Nations' key weaknesses. It did not always succeed, as the table below shows.

▼ The structure of the UN: Correcting the weaknesses of the League of Nations?

LEAGUE WEAKNESS	UNITED NATIONS REMEDY
Lack of commitment to peacekeeping	UN peacekeeping forces are supplied by their members' national armies as required. They wear blue helmets to distinguish them from other troops. In 2016 there were over 95,000 personnel from over 120 different countries working as UN peacekeepers. The Military Staff Committee advises the Council in the deployment and conduct of peacekeeping forces.
Unanimous decisions necessary to enact any resolution	The UN Security Council needs a majority of nine out of 15 to make decisions. If the decision concerns issues of international security, a simple majority is enough if all five of the permanent members vote in favour it. This gives the permanent five a right of veto, however, and they can block measures against their interests.
Not all major powers were members of the League of Nations	From the start the USA and USSR were members of the UN. All major powers are members of the UN General Assembly. The Security Council's permanent members are the USA, Russia, China, France and Great Britain. This has led to criticism, however, as circumstances have changed. Countries like Brazil and India are emerging as potential new superpowers, which are not permanent members of the Security Council.

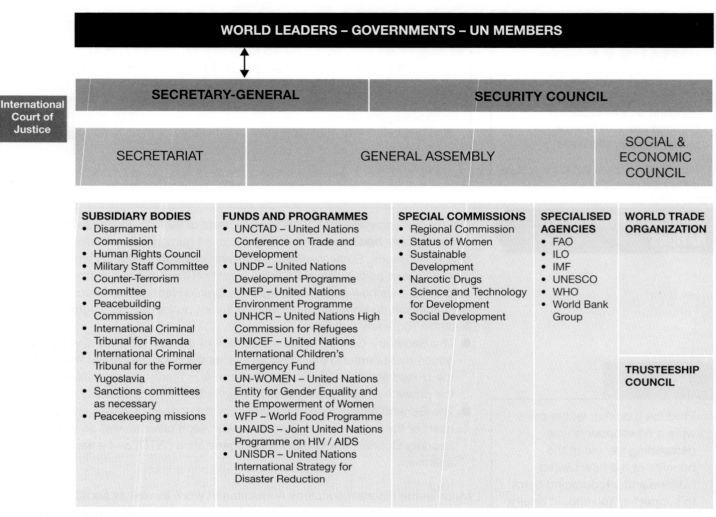

▲ Figure 3.2 Structure of the UN

STRUCTURAL PROBLEMS: THE SECURITY COUNCIL

THE SECURITY COUNCIL'S MEMBERSHIP

The way in which the UN was structured in 1945 gave western nations the greatest influence. Since then, however, the world has changed. One key criticism of the UN is that it doesn't reflect the changes in the world's population and economics. Three key reasons for this are as follows.

- When the European empires collapsed, France and Great Britain's global power declined, yet they remained on the Security Council.
- New economic powers with large populations have emerged, such as India and Brazil. They are not on the Security Council.
- There are no Latin American, African or Middle Eastern countries on the Security Council.

THE VETO

The Cold War made co-operation between the five permanent members of the Security Council impossible. Any proposal was regarded by the USA and USSR in terms of whether it would give the other an advantage in the balance of power. If so, it would be vetoed. This meant that the UN was very limited in what it could achieve.

Between 1946 and the end of the Cold War in 1991, the USSR used its veto 114 times, compared with the USA's 96 vetoes. Thirteen peacekeeping operations were authorised between 1945 and 1985, compared with 36 between 1988 and 2015. This suggests that once the Cold War ended it became easier for the permanent five to agree, making the Security Council more effective.

SOURCE C

This cartoon from 2008 illustrates that, even after the Cold War, the national interests of the permanent five limit the Security Council's, and thus the UN's, effectiveness. It concerns resolution 8888, condemning Burma's human rights record.

National interests often affect the way in which UN members vote. In the case of the permanent five of the Security Council, their veto gives them far more power to shape UN policies and actions than any other countries, as Source C shows. In the cartoon, the then UN Secretary-General, Ban Ki Moon, has made a proposal condemning the abuse of human rights by the Burmese military government. The five figures in front represent the permanent five of the Security Council. Each makes a comment that shows they will vote according to their own national interests rather than putting human rights first.

France (on the far left) will support the Secretary-General because it has no economic interest in Burma. It therefore has nothing to lose by upsetting the Burmese government.

The Russian Federation under Putin (second from left) is shown as seeing the issue as a Burmese affair and not anyone else's business. This is because, the cartoonist suggests, Putin is behaving in a similar way in the Russian province of Chechnya, where there was also unrest and human rights issues.

The USA, under its then president George W. Bush (middle figure) is happy to vote in favour of the Secretary-General's proposal because there is no oil in Burma. The cartoonist is suggesting that the USA only becomes involved in problems if it affects their economic interests, especially oil supplies. For example, American involvement in the Middle East is often viewed as being about oil supplies, not about issues such as human rights or the political stability of the region. Some believe oil was the real reason why President Bush decided to invade Iraq in 2003, for example (see pages 93–95).

On the other hand China (second from right) will vote against the Secretary-General's proposal because it is shown as a political ally of Burma.

Meanwhile, according to the cartoonist, Britain (on the far right of the picture, represented by its then prime minister, Gordon Brown) will do whatever the USA wants. Britain is often seen as having very close ties to the USA and doing whatever the USA wants. For example, it supported its invasion of Iraq in 2003.

THE SECURITY COUNCIL AND CHINA

In 1949, China had a communist revolution after a long civil war between the Chinese Communist Party and the **right wing**, American-backed nationalist Chinese government. The nationalists retreated to the island of Taiwan. In terms of the Cold War, this was a victory for the USSR.

The USSR and the new People's Republic of China expected that a representative of the new communist government would take China's permanent seat on the Security Council. This was not the case: the nationalist Chinese kept it. In effect, the fifth permanent member of the Security Council was now Taiwan, which was not a major power. The USA, France and Great Britain would not agree to any changes. It was not until 1971 that the People's Republic of China replaced Taiwan as the fifth permanent member of the Security Council. At this time, relations between China and the USA were improving, and relations between China and the USSR were worsening. This meant that China would no longer necessarily side with the USSR on the Security Council.

(see pages 93–95).

KEY TERM

align to publicly support a political group, country or person that you agree with

STRUCTURAL PROBLEMS: THE GENERAL ASSEMBLY

EXTEND YOUR KNOWLEDGE

One of the most famous incidents at the UN General Assembly was in 1960 when the leader of the USSR, Nikita Khrushchev, reacted angrily to the Philippines delegate, who spoke about how Eastern Europe had suffered under Soviet control. After first hitting the table in front of him with both fists, Khrushchev took off his right shoe and banged it with that instead. He continued until the General Assembly had stopped to watch. The most popular question asked by tourists visiting the UN in New York is, 'Where was Khrushchev sitting when he banged the table with his shoe?'

MEMBERSHIP

The USSR used its veto 75 times between 1946 and 1955. The majority of its vetoes were against countries asking to join the UN. Its concern was that too many of the new members were **aligned** with the West, giving the USA an advantage in the General Assembly as well as the Security Council. This limited the membership of the UN, especially in its first decade.

The collapse of the European empires in the second half of the 20th century led to a large increase in UN membership from newly independent countries in **Sub-Saharan Africa** and Asia. Many are LEDCs (Less Economically Developed Countries) with different problems and national interests from economically more advanced nations. This has changed the balance of power in the General Assembly away from European and developed nations. Nevertheless, because of the power of the Security Council, and the permanent five in particular, this is not necessarily reflected in the UN's policies and actions.

THE GENERAL ASSEMBLY'S ROLE

Decisions taken by the Security Council must be followed, even if the majority of the General Assembly prefers a different course of action. The General Assembly chooses the non-permanent members of the Security Council, thus giving it some influence. In less important matters the Security Council only needs a simple majority to enforce a decision, so the permanent five can be out-voted by the other ten. This means that the nations voted onto the Security Council by the General Assembly have more power in less important issues. When issues of international security are concerned, however, the permanent five must agree.

SOURCE D

German Chancellor Angela Merkel delivers a speech to the UN General Assembly in 2010.

UN PEACEKEEPING FORCES

Article 1 of the UN Charter focuses on the need for collective action to deal with threats to international peace and security. Article 2 requires all members to provide whatever assistance is necessary, which can include armed forces.

Originally it was intended that the UN would have its own military forces, with bases around the world and an air force. However, Cold War tensions ended hope of military co-operation between the Eastern and Western blocs and so no special UN military force was established.

The UN has a Military Staff Committee (UNMSC) that meets every 2 weeks. It is made up of service personnel from the permanent five as well as any UN members whose forces are currently being **deployed**. Different countries can supply personnel throughout a mission, so that the burden is shared between member states. However, often it is the larger, wealthier powers, such as the USA, that contribute most. Once a mission is finished, the forces are disbanded – although missions can last for years.

If necessary, the UNMSC also works with regional military forces such as NATO or the African Union. Nevertheless, without its own dedicated force, the UN's ability to react swiftly to a crisis is limited. This means that United Nations' peacekeeping forces often arrive just after a conflict starts rather than being deployed to prevent one.

SOURCE E

UN peacekeeping forces from Haiti protecting humanitarian aid workers after an earthquake.

EXAM-STYLE QUESTION

A01   **A02**

SKILLS   PROBLEM SOLVING, REASONING, DECISION MAKING

How far did the set-up and role of the United Nations differ from that of the League of Nations?

You may use the following in your answer:
- the Secretary-General
- peacekeeping forces.

You **must** also use information of your own.   **(16 marks)**

HINT

Although there are lots of similarities between the two organisations, such as the secretariat or the assembly, very little is exactly the same.

ACTIVITY

1 In small groups discuss what impact the make-up of the permanent members of the Security Council might have on the United Nations and its effectiveness.
2 Find as many examples as you can of the impact that (a) the Cold War and (b) decolonisation had on the United Nations.
3 In pairs or small groups, identify what changes you would make to the United Nations to make it more effective. Present your ideas to the rest of the class. As you listen to other groups' presentations, can you think of any problems with the changes they have suggested?
4 Study Source C. What does the artist suggest really influences the five permanent members of the Security Council in deciding whether to use the veto or not?

HUMAN RIGHTS COUNCIL

KEY TERMS

genocide the deliberate murder of a whole group or race of people

summit an important meeting or set of meetings between the leaders of several governments

EXTEND YOUR KNOWLEDGE

Eleanor Roosevelt was chair of the UN Human Rights Committee and was perhaps more responsible than any one other person for the Universal Declaration of Human Rights, published in 1948. She was committed to reform and believed in being actively involved, including serving in soup kitchens, going down mines or visiting slums to raise awareness of deprivation, inequality and injustice. Eleanor was famous for the energy she gave to human rights for women, children and men of all races and religions, working tirelessly before, during and after she was America's First Lady 1932–1945.

ACTIVITY

1 In pairs, decide how successful the United Nations has been in dealing with both disarmament and human rights. You should rate it on a scale of 1–6 (1 = total failure; 2 = largely a failure; 3 = more of a failure than a success; 4 = more of a success than a failure; 5 = largely a success; 6 = total success). You should list the reasons for your score.

2 Research one of the UN agencies from the diagram on page 50, other than the ODA or UNHCR. Prepare a short presentation on its aims, its work and any successes it has had.

The scale of human rights abuses during the Second World War, including systematised **genocide**, directly encouraged the development of the UN Declaration of Human Rights in 1948, and the inclusion of crimes against humanity in particular.

The Declaration is non-binding. This means states that break it cannot be punished. Even so, some nations abstained in 1948, concerned that signing the Declaration of Human Rights would enable the UN to interfere in their domestic matters.

The UN sees human rights as necessary for achieving its other aims: social and economic development and international peace and security. Led by the UN High Commissioner for Human Rights, the UNHRC works with governments, other UN agencies and international organisations to:
- promote and encourage respect for human rights for all
- identify, research and monitor human rights abuses
- provide assistance to governments, for example in administering justice and reform legislation.

The UNHRC's role developed further after the 1990s, which saw genocides in Bosnia and Rwanda, where thousands were massacred for being of a certain **ethnic origin**. In 2005 at a World **Summit** UN members agreed that the international community should take action where a government is failing to protect its own people (see page 90).

SOURCE F

A march in Karachi, Pakistan, on 9 December 2012 to mark UN Human Rights Day.

EXAM-STYLE QUESTIONS

A01   **A02**

SKILL ▶ ADAPTIVE LEARNING

Explain **two** reasons why the effectiveness of the United Nations in maintaining peace can be limited.   **(8 marks)**

HINT

The United Nations has many aims and roles. You need to be clear about which aspect of its work you have chosen to write about in your answer before explaining why it is not always effective.

▼ The work of the UN

ILO International Labour Organization	UNHRC UN Human Rights Council	UNHCR UN High Commissioner for Refugees	UNODA UN Office for Disarmament Affairs
Founded in 1919 with League of Nations	Promotes and protects human rights	Provides critical emergency care for displaced people	Started as Disarmament Commission in 1952; renamed UN Office for Disarmament Affairs in 1998
Almost all UN members belong to the ILO	Identifies breaches of human rights	Tries to ensure everyone can seek asylum and safe refuge	All UN members belong to UNODA
Promotes social justice and sets labour standards	Provides education and legal support to enforce human rights	Assists both those wanting to return home and those wanting to settle elsewhere	Promotes disarmament of all weapons of mass destruction (WMDs), landmines and chemical weapons
Develops policies and programmes promoting decent work and social protection for all	Works with governments to improve human rights	Established UN Relief and Works Agency for Palestine in 1949 (still operating)	Was tasked with overseeing Iraq's disarmament in the 1990s; its failure to deal with the issue of Iraq's WMDs was a factor in the Second Gulf War, 2003
Promotes greater opportunities for women and men to earn an income enabling a decent standard of living	Has had to deal with mass human rights abuses in many places, including Bosnia, Rwanda, Kosovo and Sudan.	Oversaw return of refugees to Namibia in 1989	
Encourages negotiation with workers		Operates around the world and has taken part in UN operations in Bosnia, Rwanda, Kosovo and Sudan.	
Promotes conditions necessary for trade unions to form and protect workers' rights in their own countries.			

FAO Food and Agriculture Organization	WHO World Health Organization	UNICEF UN International Children's Emergency Fund	UNESCO UN Educational, Scientific and Cultural Organization
Aims to eradicate hunger, food insecurity and malnutrition	Works with all UN member states	Focuses specifically on children	Focuses on moral and intellectual development programmes
Aims to eliminate poverty	Works in scores of countries across the world combatting infectious and non-infectious diseases	Agreed the UN Convention on the Rights of the Child in 1989	Promotes education for all children
Promotes sustainable management of natural resources	Delivers medicine and vaccine programmes	Works to raise awareness of, and end, dangers facing children, which it identifies as: violence, abuse, exploitation; disease, hunger, malnutrition; war and disaster	Promotes scientific co-operation
Publishes annual list of low-income, food deficient countries, where it targets its work	Monitors water, air and food quality	Works around the world and has set up missions in every conflict area studied in this text	Supports heritage and cultural diversity
Majority of FAO's work is in Sub-Saharan Africa but it also works in India, Uzbekistan and other regions.			Encourages freedom of expression
			Identifies World Heritage Sites (places that are important to the history and culture of humanity)

3.2 THE UN IN PALESTINE, 1947–49

LEARNING OBJECTIVES

- Understand how the conflict in Palestine developed
- Understand the actions taken by the United Nations to deal with the Palestinian conflict
- Explain the significance of the Palestinian conflict for the United Nations .

KEY TERM

Ottoman Empire empire founded in the 14th century centred on modern-day Turkey and at different times included parts of south-east Europe, the Middle East and parts of north Africa. It was broken up after the First World War

The Jews had occupied Palestine in Biblical times when, under the rule of ancient Rome, Jewish revolts were violently suppressed and the Jews expelled in 70 CE. In the centuries that followed, Palestine became an Arab, Muslim land and part of the **Ottoman Empire**. After the collapse of the Ottoman Empire after the First World War, Great Britain controlled Palestine by League of Nations mandate. Jewish immigration to Palestine increased in the 1920s and 30s, causing tensions with the Arab population. The **Holocaust** led to calls for Jews to have their own homeland, and in 1945 pressure increased on the British to take 100,000 Jewish settlers into Palestine. The British refused. This led to a Jewish terrorist campaign in Palestine, resulting in hundreds of deaths. With its economy weakened by years of war, Britain was increasingly unable to sustain its colonies and overseas territories. Palestine was especially expensive in both financial and military terms due to the actions of terrorist groups. In 1947, Britain asked the UN to intervene. In 1948 it left altogether.

THE UN'S PARTITION OF PALESTINE

The UN proposed the **partition** of Palestine to create two states, one Arab and one Jewish. Jerusalem, a holy place for both religions as well as for Christianity, was to be an international city under United Nations authority. The plan was passed – one occasion when there was no veto problem – but it was not unanimously popular with General Assembly member countries. The Arabs would not accept it. They said it contradicted the UN Charter's principle of self-determination; and that the plan gave **unprecedented** rights to a minority, including the handing over of large pieces of land. The violence between Arabs and Jews increased.

The state of Israel was proclaimed on 14 May 1948. The next day Iraq, Lebanon, Syria, Jordan and Egypt attacked Israel. On 29 May 1948, a UN resolution called for a **ceasefire**, which was to be supervised by a UN **mediator**, Count Folke Bernadotte of Sweden. He was assisted by military observers, the United Nations Truce Supervision Organization (UNTSO). Palestine was thus the UN's first peacekeeping mission.

The situation remained dangerous throughout 1948. No **truce** lasted for very long; Bernadotte was murdered; Israel pushed back Arab forces, although they lost control of Gaza, the West Bank and east Jerusalem; 750,000 Palestinian Arabs were made refugees.

In December 1948 the UN adopted Resolution 194 to deal with the Palestinian problem. It called for:

- refugees to be allowed to return home
- refugees who did not wish to return home to be compensated for their lost property
- Jerusalem to be demilitarised and protected access to all holy places to be guaranteed.

A UN Conciliation Commission was set up to work to resolve the dispute, but was unable to do so despite several attempts over the years. As the situation stood, the Arab states had effectively lost the conflict. In May 1949, Israel became a member of the United Nations, which in effect showed recognition of it as an independent country. The work of the UN was not finished, however, as there were around 1 million Arab refugees who fled from Israel. It set up UNRWA (the UN Relief and Works Agency for Palestinian Refugees) in 1949. Its work began in 1950 and is still ongoing in 2017.

The UN Partition of Palestine plan

• Jewish state (Israel)
Covered 56% of Palestine
Population: 498,000 Jewish; 325,000 Arabs
(60.5% Jewish; 39.5% Arab)

• Arab state (Palestine)
Covered 44% of Palestine
Population: 807,000 Arabs; 10,000 Jewish
(98.8% Arab; 1.2% Jewish)

• Jerusalem
International city under UN authority
Population: 100,000 Jewish; 105,000 Arabs

▲ Figure 3.3 UN Partition of Palestine

SIGNIFICANCE OF THE UN IN PALESTINE

The United Nations' involvement in Palestine was significant for the following reasons.
- It was the first time the UN was asked to intervene in a dispute that had the potential to threaten international peace and security.
- It lead to the UN's first peacekeeping force being established.
- The necessary resolutions passed without a veto – but this was not enough to guarantee a successful outcome.

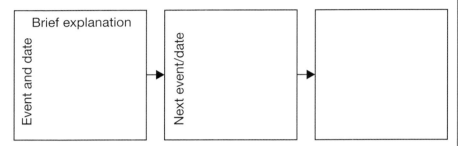

ACTIVITY

1 Draw a flow diagram (see example below) to show the build up of events leading up to the establishment of the state of Israel in 1948. Show as many events / stages as you need.

2 Identify the strategies used by the UN in dealing with the Palestinian crisis and the outcomes of those strategies. For example, mediating the dispute is a strategy.

3.3 THE UN IN KOREA, 1950–53

LEARNING OBJECTIVES

- Understand how the conflict in Korea developed
- Understand the actions taken by the United Nations to deal with the Korean conflict
- Explain the significance of the Korean conflict for the United Nations.

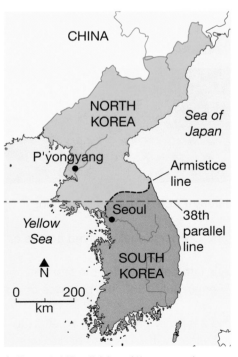

▲ Figure 3.4 The division of Korea was along the 38th parallel

When the Japanese forces occupying Korea surrendered after the Second World War, they surrendered to the USSR north of the **38th parallel** and to the USA south of it. In 1947 the UN announced elections for a new Korean government. The USSR refused to co-operate. Instead, the north set up a communist government under Kim Il Sung. The south voted in Syngman Rhee, an American ally. Both men claimed to be the rightful leader of the whole of Korea.

In June 1950, North Korea invaded South Korea. It was such an obvious case of aggression that the Security Council adopted a series of resolutions requiring North Korea's troops to withdraw, and organised UN forces to help South Korea against the communist north. These resolutions were only possible because at the time the USSR was **boycotting** the UN over the UN's refusal to recognise the new communist government of China.

As the US-led UN forces in Korea pushed back the communist forces into North Korea, the USA hoped for a new UN objective to be agreed. It wanted to destroy the communists and reunify Korea under an elected (pro-American) government. By November 1950, UN forces were close to the Chinese border. The situation had changed, however. In August 1950 the USSR had returned to the UN to take its turn at the presidency of the Security Council. And in October, the Chinese had entered the war to support Kim Il Sung's forces. The USSR would veto any resolutions either trying to develop the aims of the Korean War further or calling for the Chinese to withdraw.

To get around the problem of the USSR's veto in the Security Council, the USA used the General Assembly, where a majority supported it. The General Assembly passed Resolution 377(V). Known as the 'Uniting for Peace' resolution, it enables the General Assembly to organise a special emergency session if the Security Council has not been able to fulfil its function of maintaining international peace and security. An emergency meeting of the General Assembly can be called even if it is not in session (it meets annually every September,) if seven members of the Security Council request it. According to 377(V), the General Assembly can then make recommendations for collective action to deal with a situation, including the use of armed force if necessary.

Ultimately, the changing military situation, with UN forces being pushed back south of the 38th parallel, meant that the objectives of the Korean War would stay as they were: simply to repel North Korea and restore the boundaries between north and south. UN mediators succeeded in getting both sides to agree to an **armistice**, which came into effect in July 1953.

SIGNIFICANCE OF THE UN IN KOREA

The Korean War was significant to the development of the UN because:
- it bolstered the UN's reputation (it had stood up to an aggressor unlike the League of Nations)
- it was the first time that UN forces were deployed to a country to restore peace
- it showed that international co-operation could work if there were no veto: 16 nations had taken part on the side of South Korea
- the 'Uniting for Peace' resolution was passed, which allows the General Assembly to pass a resolution under certain circumstances when one of the five permanent members used the veto
- some nations came to see the UN as a tool of US foreign policy.

3.4 THE UN IN THE CONGO, 1960–64

LEARNING OBJECTIVES

- Understand how the conflict in the Congo developed
- Understand the actions taken by the United Nations to deal with the Congo conflict
- Explain the significance of the conflict in the Congo for the United Nations.

The UN's involvement in the Congo was different from other peacekeeping missions it had undertaken because:
- the scale was unprecedented, with 20,000 UN personnel involved across a range of activities
- it was asked to involve itself in a country's internal affairs for the first time. This was to keep the Congo together when, in July 1960, the province of Katanga tried to break away
- although it used diplomacy and deployed a military presence in an effort to protect both Congolese and international security, the UN also had to use its forces proactively, to try to prevent a full-scale war breaking out.

LEADERS INVOLVED IN THE CONGO CRISIS, 1960–64

▲ Patrice Lumumba, Prime
Minister of the Congo
1960–61

▲ Joseph Kasavubu,
President of the Congo

▲ Mobuto Sese Seko,
Commander of the
Congolese Army

▲ Moise Tshomobe, Leader of
Katanga Province

▲ Cyrille Adoula, Prime
Minister of the Congo from
1961

The Congo had been a Belgian colony until June 1960 when, after only 6 months' notice and no real preparation, it was given its independence. Belgium simply handed over power, although thousands of Belgians stayed on in both their homes and their privileged positions. For example, there were no black officers in the army, it was commanded by Belgians. For ordinary people, very little had actually changed apart from a new and inexperienced government – which was only elected the week before independence was granted. The new Congolese prime minister was Patrice Lumumba, and its president was Joseph Kasavubu.

Trouble began immediately. The army mutinied against both its Belgian officers and the new Congolese government. Brutal attacks targeted white people, leading to thousands of Belgians fleeing the Congo. Belgium therefore sent in troops to protect white Europeans, increasing the violence.

The Congolese government's position worsened when a local leader, Moise Tshombe, declared independence for the resource-rich province of Katanga. Lumumba and Kasavubu asked the United Nations to intervene. Secretary-General Hammarskjöld called a meeting of the Security Council. It agreed that UN forces (the ONUC) would go immediately to the Congo to replace Belgian troops and restore order. UN forces faced a difficult task. Replacing Belgian troops was largely successful, except in Katanga. Restoring order, however, was harder.

In September, **Prime Minster** Lumumba and President Kasavubu dismissed each other. The Congolese army's commander, Mobutu Sese Seko, then staged a military **coup**. After seizing power, he was supported by President Kasabuvu. Lumumba, however, was murdered in January 1961, after being captured by Tshombe's men.

The Congo was divided both politically and geographically. The situation risked developing into a full-scale civil war with the potential to destabilise the entire region. Forces in the Portuguese colony of Angola began a war for independence in 1961 and Tanganyika, Uganda, Kenya and Rhodesia (Zimbabwe) were all British territories in the process of gaining independence at the time. Furthermore, the Congolese civilian population was suffering as three different groups fought for power:

■ Tshombe in Katanga, supported by Belgian troops and **mercenaries**
■ Mobutu in Leopoldville, supported by President Kasabuvu
■ Lumumba's forces in Stanleyville, with the support of the USSR.

KEY TERM

secession breaking away from an organisation or country

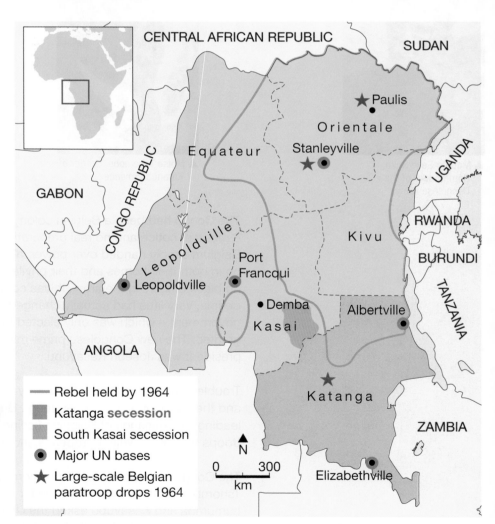

▲ **Figure 3.5** The conflict in the Congo

With the situation getting out of control, the UN authorised the ONUC to use force to restore order. One major threat was that mercenaries were being used in the Congo, especially in Katanga. It was crucial to get rid of them if there was to be a chance of stability and so, in 1961, the ONUC was ordered to capture and expel all foreign forces in Katanga. This required the UN to launch an offensive – Operation Rumpunch – rather than simply reacting to developments in order to keep the peace.

Some progress was made in the Congo as 1961 wore on.
- The Congolese in Leopoldville and Stanleyville came together under Cyrille Adoula, the new, civilian prime minister.
- The UN refused to back down, despite criticism of its new, aggressive approach. It continued with its operation even after the UN Secretary-General, Dag Hammarskjöld, was killed in a plane crash in September 1961.
- Operation Rumpunch was a successful, if very bloody, operation.
- By the end of 1962, all mercenaries had left Katanga and Tshombe left the Congo.

In 1963, Katanga was re-united with the rest of the Congo. UN forces withdrew in 1964. The success of the UN's mission was, however, short lived. President Kasavubu appointed his one-time rival, Tshombe, as prime minister of the Congo before the end of 1964. Their rivalry soon reappeared, however, and by 1965 the relationship broke down again. The Congo went on to experience many more years of rebellion and conflict.

SOURCE G

The remains of the plane in which Dag Hammarskjöld lost his life.

SIGNIFICANCE OF THE CONGO FOR THE UN

- It was the largest peacekeeping operation the UN had ever carried out.
- The UN involved itself in the internal affairs of the Congo. This went far beyond previous peacekeeping duties, which had concerned disputes between countries.
- The UN Security Council had authorised the use of force to impose peace in Katanga province.
- The UN had taken a strong stance against imperialism.

ACTIVITY

1 Make a timeline of the events in the Congo crisis 1960–64.
2 Make a chart (see the example below) comparing the UN responses to the conflicts in Korea and the Congo, and their outcomes.

UN ROLE	KOREA 1950–53	THE CONGO 1960–64
RESPONSES		
OUTCOMES		

3 Write a speech EITHER as a Soviet delegate to the United Nations General Assembly condemning the UN as a tool of US foreign policy OR as the UN Secretary-General explaining why Operation Rumpunch is necessary.

EXAM-STYLE QUESTIONS

A01   A02

Explain **two** ways in which the United Nations' approach to peacekeeping in Abyssinia (1935–36) was different from its approach in the Congo (1960–64).

(6 marks)

HINT

Think about both the nature and the circumstances of the two conflicts.

CONCLUSION

Events in Palestine, Korea and the Congo reflected wider international developments after the Second World War: refugee issues; the emergence of the concept of crimes against humanity; the Cold War; and the collapse of European empires in Africa, Asia and the Middle East. The UN had some successes, although none of the situations were fully resolved and instability in the regions involved continued.

Unlike the League of Nations, the UN had managed to employ armed forces to support its decisions. And it had implemented collective security in South Korea (although this was due to a peculiar set of circumstances). In the years to come, however, it would face conflicts that clearly showed the UN members did not always apply the ideals it represented.

RECAP

RECALL QUIZ

1 When was the United Nations established?
2 When was the UN Declaration of Human Rights issued?
3 How many countries sit on the Security Council at any one time?
4 What is the main role of the UN General Assembly?
5 What is the UNMSC?
6 Which UN agency works to get rid of hunger?
7 Which country was founded in May 1948?
8 Why did the Korean War start?
9 Which country had occupied the Congo before its independence?
10 Which province of the Congo made itself independent in 1960?

CHECKPOINT

STRENGTHEN
S1 What is the role of the UN Security Council?
S2 What made it possible for the UN to send military forces into Korea in 1950?
S3 When was the Congo reunited?

CHALLENGE
C1 Explain one key weakness in the set-up of the UN.
C2 Name three different UN agencies.
C3 Explain one way in which the UN became involved in Palestine in 1948.

SUMMARY

- The set-up of the United Nations hoped to overcome some of the League of Nations' weaknesses.
- The UN was unable to establish its own military force due to the Cold War.
- Executive power of the UN lies with the Security Council.
- The Security Council permanent five can veto important UN decisions.
- Human rights are an important focus of the United Nations' work.
- The UN proposed the division of Palestine to end the crisis there in 1948.
- The UNHCR has been working in Palestine since setting up UNRWA in 1949.
- The Korean War was the first time that the UN used military force to enforce its resolutions.
- It was only because the USSR was boycotting the UN that the decision to use military force in Korea was agreed.
- In the Congo, the UN involved itself in a country's internal affairs for the first time.

EXAM GUIDANCE: PART (C) QUESTIONS

A01 **A02**

SKILLS PROBLEM SOLVING, REASONING, DECISION MAKING

Question to be answered: How far did the United Nations' approach to peacekeeping change in the years 1947 to 1973?

You may use the following in your answer:
■ the crisis in Palestine, 1947–49
■ the Yom Kippur War, 1973.
You must also use information of your own.   **(16 marks)**

1 Analysis Question 1: What is the question type testing?
In this question you have to demonstrate that you have knowledge and understanding of the key features and characteristics of the period studied. In this particular case it is knowledge and understanding of the role of UN peacekeeping and how it developed in the years 1947–73.

You also have to explain, analyse and make judgements about historical events and periods to give an explanation and reach a judgement on the role of various factors in bringing about changes.

2 Analysis Question 2: What do I have to do to answer the question well?
You have been given two factors on which to write: you don't have to use those factors (though it might be wise to do so). You must, however, include at least one factor, other than those you have been given, such as the Korean War or the increasing role of agencies like the UNHCR that developed the work of the peacekeepers.

You are also asked 'how far' UN peacekeeping changed, so consider what stayed the same as well as what changed. Look at actual examples of UN peacekeeping to do this.

3 Analysis Question 3: Are there any techniques I can use to make it very clear that I am doing what is needed to be successful?
This is a 16-mark question and you need to make sure you give a substantial answer. You will be up against time pressures so here are some useful techniques to help you succeed.
■ Give a **brief** introduction that defines peacekeeping, points out any major changes and highlights those aspects of peacekeeping that remained the same throughout the period in question.
■ To make sure you stay focused on the question and avoid just writing narrative, try to use the words of the question at the beginning of each paragraph.
■ Link back to the question during your essay to make sure that what you are writing about explains **how far** the UN's approach to peacekeeping changed.

Answer

Here is a student response to the question. The teacher has made some comments.

Good introduction. It is clear that you understand how the UN saw peacekeeping at the time

In 1947, the UN began its first peacekeeping mission in Palestine. By the time it pulled out of the Congo in 1964, the UN saw peacekeeping as something that had human rights and social and economic aspects as well as enabling ceasefires and ensuring that they were kept.

You have clearly identified the approach taken by the UN and supported it with specific evidence. The answer is a little narrative-based in the middle, however, the last sentence gives a clear judgement.

There was a change in how the UN approached peacekeeping because of the different circumstances of its early missions. The Arabs had attacked after Israel proclaimed itself a new country on land that had been occupied by Palestinians. The UN's plan to partition Palestine was rejected by the Palestinians, so UN military observers were sent to keep the ceasefires in place. However, they could not stop Israel and the Arabs fighting. No truces lasted very long, and the UN mediator was murdered. The UN also set up a Conciliation Commission as part of its approach but it failed. As part of its peacekeeping mission, the UNHCR established refugee camps to try to support the Palestinians fleeing their homes. This first mission was much more limited than later ones.

This does mention similarities and differences but the impact of the Cold War could be developed a little more, or the Six Day War could be added or perhaps establishing and supervising a buffer zone.

There was nothing new about the methods used by the UN in the Yom Kippur War. It used resolutions, UNEF II and the UNRWA. An important change was how weak the UN was because of the Cold War. Israel thought the UN was too pro PLO and so the USA took the lead role in negotiations. The UN's peacekeepers did undertake their normal role of supervising and monitoring things, for example, the disengagement agreements.

Good concise finish that makes judgements about the change in UN peacekeeping. Perhaps a final sentence that says how far you think it changed would make sure that it links strongly back to the question?

In conclusion, the UN's peacekeeping forces grew larger and became more involved in the conflicts they were sent to deal with. The UN began to use force to enforce its resolutions in Korea, and showed it was prepared to get involved in a country's internal affairs, like in the Congo. Its aims of trying to keep international peace did not change and UN mediators continued to play an important role.

What are the strengths and weaknesses of this answer?

You can see the strengths and weaknesses of this answer from what the teacher says. If there had been three paragraphs like the one on Palestine, this would have been a very good answer. Although the Yom Kippur War was mentioned, the candidate has not used any of their own examples to develop their answer and there is nothing from the middle of the era in question.

Work with a friend

Discuss with a friend how you would turn the weaker paragraphs in the answer to ones which would enable the whole answer to get very high marks.

Challenge a friend

Use the Student Book to set a part (c) question for a friend. Then look at the answer. Does it do the following things?

☐ Identify changes
☐ Provide detailed information to support the changes
☐ Show how the short-term changes led to long-term change
☐ Provide examples other than those given in the question
☐ Address 'how far?'

4. THE UNITED NATIONS CHALLENGED, 1967–89

LEARNING OBJECTIVES

- Understand how the UN tried to deal with problems in the Middle East
- Understand the role of the UN in Lebanon
- Understand how the UN was successful in Namibia.

The UN's approach to peacekeeping changed over the years 1967–89, when it faced some very difficult challenges. It was to find the problems that existed in the Middle East, which had been an unstable region since the founding of Israel in 1948, were too complex for the UN to make a significant difference.

By 1989, it was clear that the Cold War was over. There was a mood of optimism, including hopes of the UN becoming more effective without bitter US–USSR rivalry. This was clearly shown in Namibia, where the UN played an important role in helping the country to gain independence from South Africa.

4.1 THE UN IN THE MIDDLE EAST 1967 AND 1973

LEARNING OBJECTIVES

Understand the role the UN played in the Six Day War (1967) and the Yom Kippur War (1973)

Explain the factors limiting the UN's role in both conflicts, especially the Cold War

Understand and explain the impact of these conflicts on later UN peacekeeping.

THE PROBLEM OF SECURITY COUNCIL DECISIONS

KEY TERM

capitalist someone who owns or controls a lot of money and lends it to businesses, banks, etc. to produce more wealth and make profits; someone who believes in free trade and freedom for businesses

THE COLD WAR

Relations between the USA and the USSR were difficult by the end of the war in 1945. Although they had been allies, there was now deep distrust between the **capitalist** USA and the communist USSR. By the end of 1947 this distrust had developed into the Cold War. As part of the Cold War, the USSR built up a bloc of communist countries in eastern Europe to protect itself from the West. The USA developed close ties with countries in western Europe and the Mediterranean. Both sides saw international relations as a way to show their political system was the best. One key opportunity was the break-up of the old European empires in Asia and Africa. The USA and the USSR competed for influence in the newly independent countries.

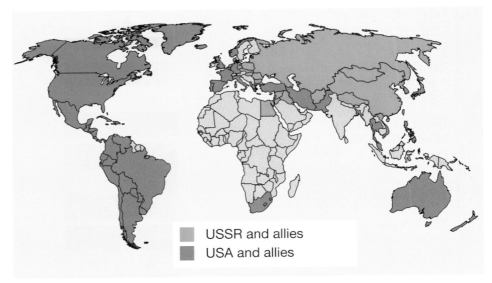

▲ **Figure 4.1** Eastern and Western blocs during the Cold War

THE VETO

The Cold War made co-operation between the five permanent members of the Security Council impossible. Any proposal was seen by both the USA and the USSR in terms of whether it would give the other an advantage in the balance of power. If so, it would be vetoed. This meant that the UN was very limited in what it could achieve, especially in international security issues. Between 1945 and 1985, only 13 peacekeeping operations were agreed (see page 81, for example).

THE SIX DAY WAR, 1967

Tensions had remained high in the Middle East after the end of the Arab–Israeli conflict in 1949, and had increased during the 1950s and 1960s. The Palestinian Liberation Organisation (PLO) was formed in 1964. Its aims included not only ending Israeli **sovereignty** in Palestine, but getting rid of the state of Israel too. The PLO was based in Jordan although it was supported by all Arab states, which helped its military forces.

PLO border raids on Israel, and Israeli retaliation, increased tensions in the Middle East. They were raised even further by fears that the superpowers would use the war as an excuse to intervene in the region. From 1956, Egypt strengthened its ties with the USSR and Israel with the USA.

In April 1967, Arab forces (including Lebanon, Syria and Jordan) began building up along their borders with Israel. In May, the Egyptian leader, Colonel Nasser, closed the Straits of Tiran to Israeli shipping, which reduced Israel's ability to trade and get oil. Israel decided that it had to take action and launched an air attack on Egypt on 5 June 1967. The Six Day War had begun.

THE SIX DAY WAR

Israel attacked by Egypt, Jordan, Syria

Egypt prepares for war
16 May 1967
Egypt warns the UN to withdraw its peacekeeping forces from its territory.

22 May 1967
Egypt blocks Israel's access to the Gulf of Aqaba by closing the Straits of Tiran to Israeli shipping.

Israel attacks Egypt
Monday, 5 June 1967
Israel launches a pre-emptive strike on grounded Egyptian and Arab air forces. It destroys over four hundred aircraft belonging to Egypt, Jordan, Syria and Iraq.

The UN reacts
Tuesday, 6 June 1967
The UN Security Council unanimously backs a ceasefire resolution. Israel rejects it.

Jordan defeated
Wednesday, 7 June 1967
Israel defeats Jordan's forces, taking the West Bank and the Arab sector of Jerusalem. Many Palestinians flee.

The UN Security Council adopts another ceasefire resolution.

Egypt defeated
Thursday, 8 June 1967
Israel crosses the Sinai Peninsula. It traps

Egyptian forces in the desert and reaches the Suez Canal.

Egypt accepts the UN's latest ceasefire resolution.

Another ceasefire resolution
Friday, 9 June 1967
The Security Council passes another ceasefire resolution. Syria accepts it but Israel rejects it.

Israel wins Six Day War
Saturday, 10 June 1967
Israel defeats Syria and takes control of the Golan Heights. It is well placed to advance towards Damascus, the Syrian capital.

Israel has strengthened its borders considerably and now controls all of Jerusalem.

Hundreds of Palestinians have fled areas now occupied by Israeli armed forces.

The UN Security Council passes another ceasefire resolution, which Israel adopts.

The way to a lasting peace?
Wednesday, 22 November 1967
The UN passes Resolution 242. It sets out proposals for finding a lasting peace in the Middle East:

• Israeli forces were to withdraw from recently taken territory.
• All states in the region were to accept each other's borders and political independence.
• Swedish diplomat Gunnar Janning was appointed as the UN's special envoy to the Middle East

▲ Figure 4.2 Account of the Six Day War

THE UN AND THE SIX DAY WAR

▲ **Figure 4.3** Land gained by Israel in the Six Day War

UN agencies had been involved in the region since 1948, and a UN Emergency Force (UNEF I) began peacekeeping duties in November 1956. However, the Egyptian leader Colonel Nasser demanded that the United Nations' peacekeeping force withdraw from Egypt in May 1967. So, although UN Secretary-General U Thant tried to use diplomacy to prevent the outbreak of war, he was unsuccessful.

The UN Security Council approved a ceasefire resolution the day after the war broke out. Israel refused to agree to it and on 7 June it took both the West Bank and the Arab section of Jerusalem. Ignoring a second ceasefire resolution, Israeli forces then moved quickly across the Sinai desert to the Suez Canal, defeating Egypt. Egypt now accepted the ceasefire, but Israel had been too successful to want to stop. A third ceasefire resolution was accepted by Syria on 9 June. The Israelis, however, continued and defeated Syria on 10 June.

The Six Day War was a great success for Israel, which had quickly defeated Egypt, Syria and Jordan. It took control of 70,000 square kilometres of land, destroyed over 800 tanks and 430 aircraft and killed 20,000 Arab soldiers. The Israelis lost just 779 men. In 6 days, Israel had strengthened its borders and its hold on Jerusalem. It agreed to the next ceasefire. The table below summarises the outcome of the Six Day War.

ACTIVITY

Your friend says to you that they think the Six Day War was a disaster for the United Nations. You don't agree. Ask them to make a list of all the reasons why it was a disaster. Tell them you will take the list and prove them wrong. See if you can!

UNITED NATIONS	ISRAEL	EGYPT
UNEF I failed in its peacekeeping duties	Was aligned with the USA	Was aligned with the USSR
Security Council was divided (USA and USSR)	Relations with the UN became strained – Israel believed the UN to be sympathetic to the Palestinian cause	Demanded UNEF I withdraw from Egyptian territory
Security Council passed ceasefire resolutions, which were initially ignored but then complied with	Refused to allow UNEF I to redeploy on its territory	Sidelined the UN by dealing with UNEF I governments directly when demanding their withdrawal
Security Council put together Resolution 242, which was passed by the United Nations	Ignored ceasefire resolutions until it had defeated its enemies and strengthened its borders	Threatened war when the UN tried to blockade the Gulf of Aqaba
UNRWA opened ten more camps to cope with Palestinians fleeing land taken by Israeli troops	Would only negotiate implementation of Resolution 242 directly with the Arab nations, not through the UN	Accepted UN ceasefire

EXTEND YOUR KNOWLEDGE

At the 1972 Munich Olympic Games, a Palestinian terrorist group known as Black September took 11 members of the Israeli team hostage. They demanded the release of 234 prisoners held by Israel. Seventeen people were killed as a result: 11 Israelis, 5 terrorists and a German policeman. The Israeli secret service, Mossad, responded by assassinating several leading Palestinian militants over the following years in what was known as Operation Wrath of God.

RESOLUTION 242

Over the summer of 1967 the Security Council worked on Resolution 242, which aimed to achieve permanent peace in the region. It was passed in November 1967 and stated that:

- Israeli forces were to withdraw from territory they had taken in recent conflicts
- all states in the region were to accept each other's borders, territory, independence and the right to live in peace
- there should be a 'just' settlement of the refugee problem.

Resolution 242 did not solve the problems in the region, however.

The Palestinians rejected it because it did not give them the right to return to the land they owned before the formation of Israel. It did not provide the homeland planned in the UN's proposals after the 1948 conflict (see page 58) either. In fact, the UNRWA had to open another ten camps for Palestinians who had escaped Israeli forces during the Six Day War.

Israel said it would negotiate separately with Egypt, Jordan and Syria. This was not possible because in August 1967 the Arab states (including Egypt, Jordan and Syria) agreed that there should be no peace with Israel, no recognition of Israel and no negotiations with Israel. Although Egypt's president, Nasser, said he would accept Resolution 242, he would only do so if Israel withdrew from all the territories it had taken in the war. Israel refused and so the resolution had little impact.

The PLO continued to attack Israel, and Arab–Israeli relations remained tense, eventually leading to another war in 1973.

THE YOM KIPPUR WAR, 1973

In 1973 the new Egyptian president, Anwar Sadat, together with the leaders of Syria and Jordan, planned to launch an attack on Israel. It was launched on Yom Kippur, which is the most important religious holiday of the year in Israel. On the day of Yom Kippur Israeli businesses were closed, the streets were empty and the synagogues full. Many Israeli soldiers were at home on leave with their families. The Israelis were taken completely by surprise. Israel was attacked in the west by Egypt, whose troops crossed the Suez Canal, and in the north by Syria, which occupied the Golan Heights.

However, the Israelis quickly recovered. Within a week they had pushed the Syrians out of the Golan Heights and had begun attacking Syria. Within 3 weeks the Egyptians had also been defeated.

6 October Israel is attacked by Egypt in the Sinai Peninsula and Syria in the Golan Heights

16 October Israel establishes a strong position on the west bank of the Suez Canal

25 October Israel cuts off Egyptian forces on the western front, and controls the northern front, of the Yom Kippur War. A successful ceasefire is negotiated by US Secretary of State, Henry Kissinger. The UN Security Council establishes UNEF II to supervise Resolution 340

13 October Israeli forces begin to reach Arab frontlines in strength

22 October Israel now occupies a 40-km-long, 32-km-wide stretch of the Suez Canal. An armistice was declared, but fighting continued. The UN passes resolution 338 calling for an end to the Yom Kippur War

ACTIVITY

1 In pairs, make a ten-question quiz on the Six Day War and how it ended. The aim is to test other students' knowledge of the events. You could use multiple choice, true / false, short answer or mix 'n' match questions. Make sure you write an answer sheet too. Swap quizzes and try someone else's, then swap back and mark them.

2 List as many reasons as you can why the UN was not able to find lasting peace between Egypt and Israel during the 1950s and 1960s.

3 Research and review what had changed for Israel between 1948 and 1973. Write up your findings or make them into a slide presentation or poster.

THE UN AND THE YOM KIPPUR WAR

The UN was unable to prevent the Yom Kippur War because none of the countries involved were prepared to listen to it. Israel did not have much faith in the UN, believing it to be sympathetic to the Palestinian cause, and so it turned to the USA for support. Egypt and the other Arab states tended to turn to the USSR.

The UN had difficulties ending the Yom Kippur War too. On 22 October 1973 the UN passed Resolution 338, calling for an end to hostilities. President Sadat agreed to the ceasefire, but the Israelis were advancing rapidly and ignored it.

On 25 October the UN passed Resolution 340 demanding another ceasefire. By this time the USSR was threatening to send troops to help Egypt, and the Arab states had stopped selling oil to the USA. They knew this would make the USA put pressure on Israel to agree to the ceasefire. It did. The USA sent its secretary of state, Henry Kissinger, to the region. Israel, which had already taken control of the conflict, agreed to stop fighting.

THE UN IN THE YOM KIPPUR WAR

NEGATIVES FOR THE UN	POSITIVES FOR THE UN
Resolution 242 (1967) did not prevent the Yom Kippur War.	UN Resolution 340, calling for an end to the Yom Kippur War on 25 October 1973, did help the fighting to end.
UN Resolution 338, calling for an end to the Yom Kippur War on 22 October 1973, was ineffective and the fighting continued.	Resolution 340 established a second emergency force, UNEF II in October 1973. It played an important role in supervising and monitoring the disengagement agreements of 1974.
It was US Secretary of State Kissinger who negotiated the deals to end the fighting on 25 October 1973.	During UNEF II's 6-year deployment, there was no further war between Israel and its Arab neighbours.
Disengagement agreements between Israel, Egypt and Syria were also negotiated by Kissinger in 1974.	
Israel increasingly ignored the UN after the Yom Kippur War, especially after the UN voted to accept the Palestinians' right to self-determination In November 1974.	

SOURCE A

UN forces replacing Israeli troops in Suez City, January 1974.

Resolution 340 established a second UN Emergency Force, UNEF II, to oversee the disengagement and supervise a **buffer zone**. There was also a UN Disengagement Observation Force to supervise Israel and Syria.

It was also Kissinger who achieved the 'disengagement agreements' between Israel and Egypt and Israel and Syria in 1974. These agreements covered the terms for forces to separate, for prisoners of war to be exchanged and for Israel to withdraw from parts of the land it had recently taken.

KEY TERM

buffer zone a piece of land separating territory occupied by different forces

THE YOM KIPPUR WAR AND PEACEKEEPING GUIDELINES

Guidelines were created for UNEF II's operations after the Yom Kippur War. Dag Hammarskjöld developed these guidelines and Secretary-General Kurt Waldheim set them out as a code for all UN peacekeeping forces to follow.

ACTIVITY

1 Write a report for the commander of UNEF II as if you had been the commander of UNEF I. What problems did you encounter? What lessons did you learn? What changes might need to be made? You can include maps, pictures, diagrams and charts in your report.

2 Which was more successful for the UN, the Six Day War or the Yom Kippur War? Explain your reasons with reference to specific events.

Principles of peacekeeping

- Peacekeepers can only be deployed with the consent of those involved in the dispute.

- Peacekeepers can only use force in self defence.

- The Security Council must offer continual support to the peacekeepers.

- Peacekeepers must remain neutral.

- All member states must be prepared to contribute personnel as well as other military resources.

A01   **A02**

SKILL   ADAPTIVE LEARNING

Explain **two** causes of the UN's inability to settle the Middle East problem in 1967.   **(8 marks)**

HINT

There are several factors that you could pick. Choose the ones that you can explain most precisely, using factual evidence to support your points.

4.2 THE UN AND LEBANON, 1975–85

LEARNING OBJECTIVES

- Understand what caused the conflict in Lebanon 1975–85
- Evaluate the role the UN played in Lebanon
- Explain the factors limiting the UN's success in Lebanon.

LEBANON: A DIVIDED NATION

The civil war in Lebanon was problematic for the UN for several reasons.
- UN peacekeeping forces could only be asked in with the agreement of all parties involved, and they had to remain neutral. This was difficult because it was a civil war and the people were divided against themselves. This meant not everyone in Lebanon wanted peacekeeping forces there.
- There were different Muslim and Christian militia groups and commanders, as well as the PLO, so working with those involved to keep the peace would be complicated.
- Syria and Israel became involved in Lebanon. They were not on friendly terms themselves and so there was the possibility for the civil war to become more serious if it were not dealt with correctly.

Lebanon was founded as a Christian nation after the First World War, although it had a large Muslim population too. Tension between the Christian and Muslim populations of Lebanon grew after the Second World War. Large numbers of Palestinians arrived in 1948 and again in the early 1970s, after Jordan told the PLO to leave its territory. By the 1970s the majority of the population was Muslim and the Christians were a minority, although a large one.

As relations between Christians and Muslims became more tense, each side developed its own political groups and militias. In the capital, Beirut, different religions lived in different quarters of the city, such as the Christians in the east and the Muslims in the west.

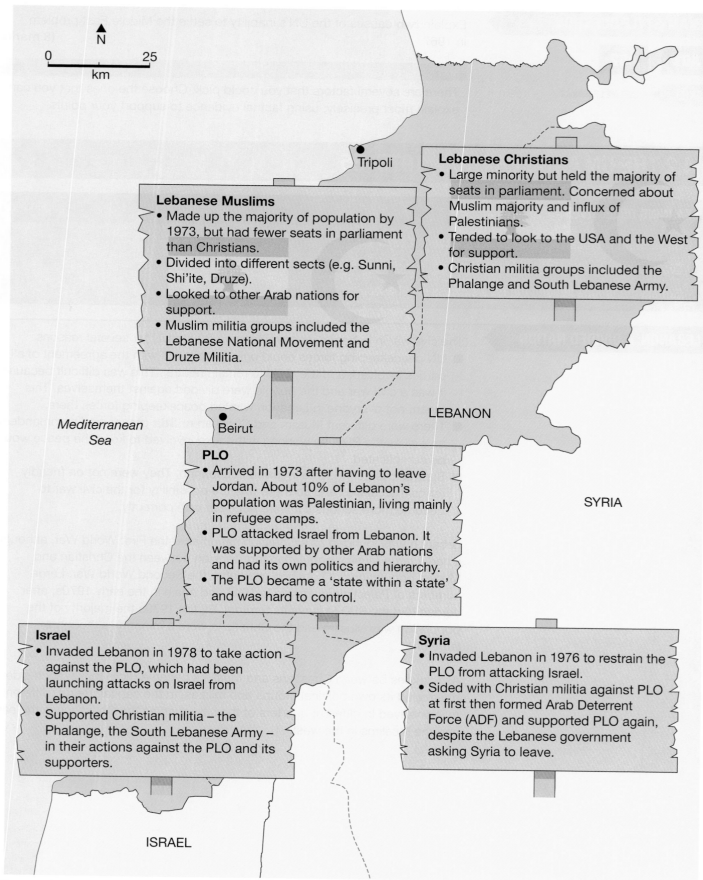

Lebanese Christians
• Large minority but held the majority of seats in parliament. Concerned about Muslim majority and influx of Palestinians.
• Tended to look to the USA and the West for support.
• Christian militia groups included the Phalange and South Lebanese Army.

Lebanese Muslims
• Made up the majority of population by 1973, but had fewer seats in parliament than Christians.
• Divided into different sects (e.g. Sunni, Shi'ite, Druze).
• Looked to other Arab nations for support.
• Muslim militia groups included the Lebanese National Movement and Druze Militia.

PLO
• Arrived in 1973 after having to leave Jordan. About 10% of Lebanon's population was Palestinian, living mainly in refugee camps.
• PLO attacked Israel from Lebanon. It was supported by other Arab nations and had its own politics and hierarchy.
• The PLO became a 'state within a state' and was hard to control.

Israel
• Invaded Lebanon in 1978 to take action against the PLO, which had been launching attacks on Israel from Lebanon.
• Supported Christian militia – the Phalange, the South Lebanese Army – in their actions against the PLO and its supporters.

Syria
• Invaded Lebanon in 1976 to restrain the PLO from attacking Israel.
• Sided with Christian militia against PLO at first then formed Arab Deterrent Force (ADF) and supported PLO again, despite the Lebanese government asking Syria to leave.

Tripoli

Mediterranean Sea

Beirut

LEBANON

SYRIA

ISRAEL

N
0   25
km

▲ Figure 4.4 Lebanon: Divisions and Occupiers

CIVIL WAR

EXTEND YOUR KNOWLEDGE

In summer 1976, the Syrian army joined with the Christian militia in a siege of the Tel al-Zaatar refugee camp. It was believed to be a PLO stronghold. After a long siege, on 12 August its inhabitants surrendered and the camp was destroyed. As they were evacuated, at least 1,500 of the refugees were killed. Those who survived were relocated to a Lebanese village called Damour. The village had been the site of a massacre of almost 150 Christians by the PLO a few months before.

Tension both within Lebanon and along its border with Israel rose during the early 1970s because:

■ the PLO attacked Israeli targets from Lebanon
■ Lebanese Christian and Muslim militias also increasingly came into conflict.

In April 1975 a long and bitter civil war began after Christian militia attacked a bus full of Palestinians after an alleged Palestinian attack on a church. The Lebanese army soon lost control, and many of its soldiers joined militia groups. In June 1976 the Syrian army invaded to restore peace and to hold back the PLO. Syria feared that PLO attacks on Israel would prompt another war in the Middle East and it would get drawn in.

In October 1976, the Arab League approved a 30,000 strong Arab Deterrent Force (which included 27,000 from Syria) to go to Lebanon to bring about a ceasefire. Lebanon protested, but was ignored.

Lebanon was invaded again on 14 and 15 March 1978 and the south of the country was occupied. This invasion was by Israel, which wanted to stop PLO attacks against it from inside Lebanon. After it invaded, Israel made an alliance with a Christian militia group, the South Lebanese Army (SLA).

ACTIVITY

1 Work in pairs with a partner. List as many possible problems as you can that the UN would face when it intervened in Lebanon.
2 Why might solutions be hard for the UN to find? List as many reasons as you can.

UNIFIL: UN INTERIM FORCES IN LEBANON

Lebanon protested to the United Nations about Israel's invasion and occupation of its land. The Security Council passed resolutions 425 and 426 on 19 March 1978. Resolution 425 required Israel to withdraw and for Lebanon's independence to be respected. Resolution 426 established UNIFIL, which was to:

■ confirm the withdrawal of Israeli forces
■ restore international peace and security in the region
■ help the Lebanese government to restore its authority over Lebanon.

UNIFIL troops began arriving in Lebanon on 23 March 1978. On 13 June 1978, Israeli forces withdrew – but they gave the areas they controlled to their allies the SLA rather than to UNIFIL. So, although progress had been made with Resolution 425 because Israel had withdrawn from Lebanon, the UN was also weakened because UNIFIL had been ignored. Coming after another SLA attack on UNIFIL that killed eight UN personnel, Israel's actions showed no respect for the United Nations. There were several more attacks too, carried out by both the PLO and SLA. Clearly, little progress had been made towards enforcing Resolution 426.

Neither UNIFIL nor the SLA was able to control southern Lebanon. Meanwhile, the PLO continued attacking Israel, which it started shelling in 1979. Israel accused the UN of being sympathetic to the PLO.

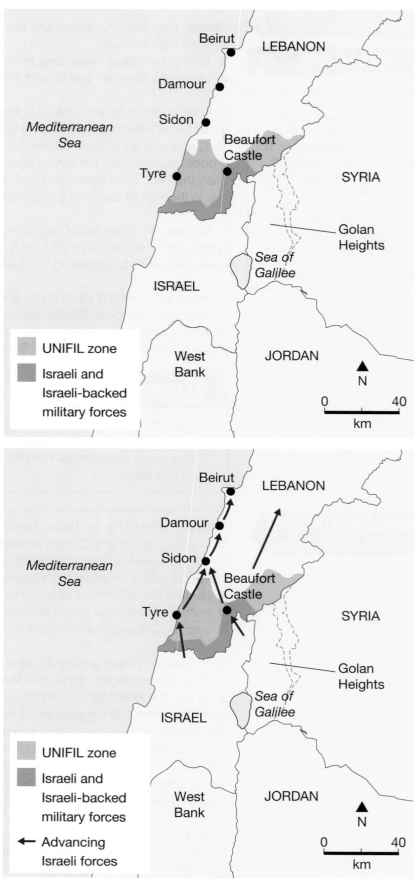

▲ Figure 4.5 UNIFIL zone in Lebanon 1978 and Israeli invasion of 1982

1982 ISRAEL INVADES AGAIN

UNIFIL remained in Lebanon, but its role was limited to offering humanitarian assistance and providing protection in the areas they were able to reach. Violence in and around Lebanon increased again in 1981–82. The PLO shelled the Israelis; the Israelis bombed the Lebanese capital, Beirut, and attacked Syrian forces. The Syrians responded with surface-to-air missiles.

Israel invaded Lebanon again on 6 June 1982, breaking Resolution 425. It ignored UNIFIL completely and reached Beirut. UNIFIL was now stuck behind Israeli lines. It did what it could, but any hope of applying resolutions 425 and 426 was gone. Seeking assistance, Lebanon turned to a multinational force led by the Americans instead. This further highlighted the UN's weakness in Lebanon.

LEBANON 1982

DATE	KEY EVENTS	UN'S ROLE
6 June 1982	Israel invaded Lebanon again. It reached Beirut by 14 June.	UNIFIL remained behind Israeli lines, where it had been for 3 years. Its role was limited to providing protection and humanitarian assistance to local people as far as it was able. Other UN organisations were also present in Lebanon, such as UNICEF.
July 1982	The PLO said it would leave Beirut if a multinational force were brought in to protect Palestinian civilians.	
Aug–Sep 1982	Multinational forces begin arriving – mainly US plus some French and Italian troops.	
1 Sep 1982	By this time, over 14,000 armed PLO forces had left Beirut; PLO headquarters were transferred to Tunis, Tunisia – but the war in Lebanon continued.	The Secretary-General continued trying to persuade Israel to withdraw, but the Israelis' relationship with the UN was difficult.

EXTEND YOUR KNOWLEDGE

White phosphorus is also known as 'Willie Pete'. It is toxic, highly flammable, gives off an intense light and creates a great deal of smoke. It can be used in war for signalling, to mark enemy targets, or to create a smoke-screen for confusing the enemy. When it comes into contact with human skin, it will burn through to the bone. It is also poisonous. In Lebanon, Israeli forces used white phosphorus shells, which are outlawed by the UN. It lost them a great deal of international sympathy.

The situation continued getting worse, and in March 1984 the USA withdrew its troops from Lebanon after several attacks against them. In 1985 Israel decided to withdraw from Lebanon. Its decision was not made through or with the United Nations, however. It withdrew for a range of reasons.

- Public opinion was changing: the war in Lebanon was increasingly unpopular with Israelis because of continued attacks on its troops, many of whom were young conscripts doing compulsory military service.
- Israel's economy: Israel had severe economic problems and continuing with a costly war was making them much worse.
- Political changes: an unpopular war in Lebanon combined with economic problems led to a change of government in September 1984. The new government included many more moderate ministers from a range of political parties.

Israeli troops completed a phased withdrawal from Lebanon in June 1985 and created a 15-kilometre-wide security zone in southern Lebanon controlled by Israel and the SLA. This was to provide a buffer for Israel to protect it from terrorist attacks.

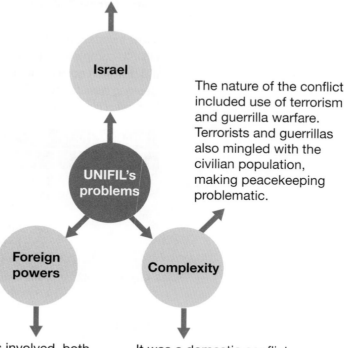

Israel believed the UN to be pro-Palestinian. It did not have a good relationship with the UN. The Secretary-General tried to persuade Israel to withdraw, but it refused.

Israel

UNIFIL's problems

The nature of the conflict included use of terrorism and guerrilla warfare. Terrorists and guerrillas also mingled with the civilian population, making peacekeeping problematic.

Foreign powers

Complexity

The parties involved, both within Lebanon and from other countries, had stronger relationships with other powers, such as the USA, the Arab League and the USSR, than with the UN.

It was a domestic conflict with foreign intervention, political and religious groups, numerous militias, plus intervention from Israel and Syria.

▲ Figure 4.6 Why the UN did not succeed in Lebanon

4.3 THE UN AND NAMIBIA

LEARNING OBJECTIVES

- Explain why there was conflict concerning Namibia
- Understand the role the UN played in Namibia
- Explain the factors impacting upon the success of the UN in Namibia.

SOUTH AFRICA, NAMIBIA AND THE UN

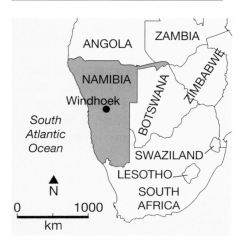

▲ Figure 4.7 Namibia

KEY TERM

apartheid a social and political system in South Africa strictly enforced by harsh laws that separated people according to race

South Africa had occupied South-West Africa (as Namibia was then called) under a League of Nations mandate since 1920. After the Second World War it refused to co-operate with the new United Nations, which wanted South-West Africa's independence. Instead, South Africa continued its occupation.

In 1960 the South West African People's Organisation (SWAPO) was created to campaign for the country's independence from South Africa. SWAPO was recognised by the UN as the legitimate representative of the Namibian people. However, the South African regime refused to negotiate with what it called a terrorist organisation. After South Africa ignored a United Nations order to withdraw in 1966, SWAPO turned to armed conflict to achieve its aims.

The UN General Assembly had seen a large rise in membership as many new countries were created after the collapse of the old European empires after the Second World War. Many of these new countries supported Namibia's efforts to liberate itself from South Africa.

UN opposition to South Africa was not only concerned with its occupation of Namibia, however. South Africa operated a system of strict apartheid which ignored every part of the UN Declaration of Human Rights (which South Africa had not signed). Although the General Assembly of the UN wanted economic sanctions imposed on South Africa because of apartheid, the USA and Britain used their Security Council veto to prevent this. This veto was partly due to the Cold War: South Africa was a useful ally for the West in Africa. It was also argued that economic sanctions would hit the poorest South Africans hardest, and that meant the country's black population.

NAMIBIA AND THE COLD WAR

Another problem that affected progress in Namibia was the Cold War. There had been civil war in neighbouring Angola since the 1970s. One side, the People's Movement for the Liberation of Angola (MPLA), was backed by the USSR and Cuba. The USA and South Africa backed the other side, the pro-western National Union for the Total Independence of Angola (UNITA), because they were worried about communist influence in the region. This was another reason why economic sanctions had been vetoed – if hit with sanctions, South Africa would not have been able to help fund and support UNITA.

Angola was also an issue because SWAPO used it as a base for guerrilla warfare in Namibia. Guerrilla activities were carried out by SWAPO's military force, the People's Liberation Army of Namibia (PLAN). South Africa therefore attacked Angola by land and from the air.

NAMIBIA UNDER SOUTH AFRICAN RULE

During its occupation of Namibia, South Africa developed apartheid there too. It used a variety of methods to control the Namibian people, including the use of South Africa Defence Forces (SADF). The SADF was a **counterinsurgency** unit whose main role was to deal with SWAPO and its supporters. The SADF used violence, intimidation and torture to do this. Thousands of Namibians fled to bordering states, either to join SWAPO or simply because life was so dreadful in their own country.

KEY TERM

counterinsurgency action taken against a rebel movement that wants to overthrow the government

EXTEND YOUR KNOWLEDGE

Methods used by the SADF included detention without trial; torture, including sleep deprivation, beatings, electric shocks, burns; mass detentions; curfews; rape; and 'cash for corpses' policy – money for killing opponents. Bodies and body parts were often shown as trophies to frighten people. These methods were used against civilians as well as SWAPO members. Similar methods were used in South Africa against political opponents under the apartheid regime.

PROGRESS TOWARDS A SOLUTION

During the 1980s the United Nations Secretary-General, Javier Pérez de Cuéllar, travelled throughout southern Africa organising negotiations. By December 1988, enough progress had been made for South Africa to agree to a ceasefire from 1 April 1989. This was a breakthrough; South Africa had not agreed to co-operate with the UN before as it thought that the UN was too sympathetic to SWAPO.

According to the agreement:
- South Africa would co-operate with the UN concerning both elections in Namibia and its independence
- Cuba would withdraw troops from Angola
- Angola agreed to UN observers to monitor the withdrawal of Cuban troops from its territory.

It is also true that, despite Secretary-General Pérez de Cuéllar's hard work, changing circumstances played perhaps the biggest role in finding a solution to the issue of Namibian independence.

WHAT WAS CHANGING IN 1989?

THE COLD WAR WAS ENDING
As Cold War hostilities were ending by 1989, there was much less need for the USA to have South African support in south-western Africa. The USSR was also stopping its support for overseas communist parties, including in Cuba and Angola.

INTERNATIONAL ANGER AT SOUTH AFRICA WAS REACHING NEW LEVELS
Many countries were angry about apartheid and had imposed sanctions against South Africa even though the Security Council had not made them compulsory. This was damaging its economy. Also, politically South Africa was very isolated because other nations did not want close relations with it.

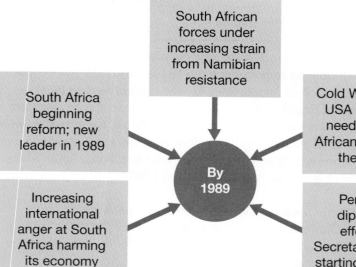

▲ Figure 4.8 What had changed by 1989?

SOUTH AFRICAN POLITICS WERE CHANGING

There was a growing demand for reform within South Africa itself during the 1980s. Black South Africans had been protesting and resisting the government for decades. By the late 1980s, their support in South Africa among the white population and in the world beyond had also grown greatly. In 1989 a new South African leader, F.W. de Klerk, took over and began to bring in reforms to end apartheid.

SOUTH AFRICAN FORCES IN NAMIBIA WERE UNDER INCREASING STRAIN

Many of South Africa's forces were involved in Namibia at a time when they were also needed to deal with instability in their own country. In addition, South African casualties in Namibia were increasing and so public opinion was turning against their involvement there.

THE UN'S ROLES IN NAMIBIA

The UN Transition Assistance Group (UNTAG) was created to oversee Namibia's independence and help build the necessary framework for a democratic state. It had three main tasks:

- disarming SADF and SWAPO troops
- monitoring the SADF withdrawal from Namibia
- demobilising Namibian armed units that had fought against SWAPO; there were about 32,500 soldiers to disarm, but the actual number was uncertain as they were mainly guerrillas.

The UNHCR was also involved. The UNHCR was to enable a peaceful return with a full **amnesty** for all Namibian refugees who wanted it. It helped thousands of Namibians to do this.

UNCIVPOL

The UN also set up UNCIVPOL (UN Civil Police) not only to help peacekeeping in Namibia, but to help create a democratic state. UNCIVPOL was to make sure that:

- the law was enforced **impartially** while it trained a new Namibian police force
- people could express their views without fear of violence or threats
- the elections were free and fair.

Although UN police had been used twice before, this was the first time UNCIVPOL had been employed on such a large scale. Its success in Namibia led to it becoming an important part of many UN operations in the 1990s, including Mozambique (see pages 107–108). This was because the aims of UN operations were changing. Rather than simply peacekeeping, the UN took a more active role in building peace within nations.

1989: A YEAR OF SETBACKS AND PROGRESS

31 March Fighting between SWAPO and South Africa forces breaks out

26 April A ceasefire starts, although between 300 and 400 people had died

1 November South Africa tries to derail Namibia's elections

22 November The last South African troops leave Namibia

1 April The ceasefire is supposed to start but doesn't

June Thousands of Namibian refugees begin returning to their homeland

7–11 November Namibia's general election for a Constituent Assembly is held

Despite the progress made, there were setbacks in the peace process in 1989. On 31 March, fighting broke out again. It took until 26 April for the situation to be brought under control. Part of the problem was that there hadn't been enough UN troops in Namibia when the ceasefire had begun.

The UNHCR organised the return of thousands of Namibian refugees. This began in June 1989 as part of the preparations for a Constituent Assembly. The Constituent Assembly would create a constitution for an independent Namibia.

Despite attempts by South Africa to prevent Namibia's elections, they went ahead between 7 and 11 November with a 97 per cent turnout. The Constituent Assembly elected SWAPO leader Sam Nujoma as president of Namibia in February 1990. Namibia finally became an independent state on 21 March 1990.

THE UN IN NAMIBIA

ACHIEVEMENTS / SUCCESSES	LIMITATIONS / FAILURES
UNTAG set up regular meetings between the parties involved in Namibia to deal with tensions as they arose. Overall there was a reduction in violence. UNTAG was well organised throughout Namibia, both in local and regional centres; this enabled the elections to go ahead smoothly. Election turnout was 97%.	UN troop levels were set originally at 7,500 but only 4,500 were ever sent due to disagreements over funding at the UN; these disagreements continued until March 1989, so on 1 April 1989 (the official start of the ceasefire) only 300 UNTAG observers were in place. In the run-up to elections there were claims that intimidation, harassment and violent acts were committed by both sides. Thirty-three UNTAG personnel were killed during the mission.

THE SIGNIFICANCE OF THE UN IN NAMIBIA

Secretary-General Javier Pérez de Cuéllar was developing a new kind of peacekeeping in Namibia. Traditionally, peacekeepers were sent to supervise ceasefires. UNTAG had a much wider role. The UN not only helped Namibia become independent, but also to successfully build a democratic government that could last, for example through UNCIVPOL's work.

ACTIVITY

1 Make a list of the problems the UN encountered in Namibia.
2 Find a partner and swap lists. Explain whether the UN was able to deal with these problems successfully. If so, how? If not, why not?
3 In small groups, make a presentation explaining why the UN was eventually able to achieve a successful outcome in Namibia. You must show which reasons were down to the UN itself and which were due to changing circumstances.

EXAM-STYLE QUESTION

A01   **A02**

SKILL   PROBLEM SOLVING, REASONING, DECISION MAKING

How far did UN peacekeeping change between 1967 and 1989?

You may use the following in your answer:
■ the UN's role in the Six Day War
■ the UN in Namibia.
You **must** also use information of your own.

(16 marks)

HINT

Do not write about all of the conflicts between these two dates. If a conflict does not show anything that will help you to answer the question, do not include it.

RECAP

RECALL QUIZ

1 What difference did the break-up of the old European empires make to the UN General Assembly?
2 With which countries did Israel and Egypt align themselves?
3 Give the start and end dates of the Six Day War.
4 Which Egyptian president started the Yom Kippur War?
5 What was the name of the UN peacekeeping force in the Yom Kippur War?
6 What was the political group attacking Israel from Lebanon?
7 What did UNIFIL stand for?
8 What were the years that Israel invaded Lebanon?
9 What does SWAPO stand for?
10 Give one of UNTAG's tasks in Namibia.

CHECKPOINT

STRENGTHEN

S1 Give one point from UN Resolution 242 and one from UN Resolution 338.
S2 Which two countries invaded Lebanon?
S3 Which country was illegally occupying Namibia?

CHALLENGE

C1 Explain why Israel accepted a ceasefire resolution on 10 June 1967.
C2 Give one reason why Israel withdrew from Lebanon in 1985.
C3 Explain one reason why the UN was able to make progress in Namibia.

SUMMARY

- The Cold War made UN peacekeeping activities more difficult.
- UN calls for a ceasefire during the Six Day War failed until the sixth day.
- The UN passed two key resolutions on the Middle East: 242 and 338.
- Clear peacekeeping guidelines were laid down after the Yom Kippur War.
- No solution to the Palestinian problem was achieved.
- UNIFIL was the UN's peacekeeping force in Lebanon.
- UNIFIL's efforts in Lebanon were severely limited.
- Israel's decision to leave Lebanon was made without the UN.
- The ending of the Cold War played an important part in the UN's success in Namibia.
- The UN's peacekeeping approach to Namibia was different because it stayed after the ceasefire to oversee the elections and the change to a democratic government.

EXAM GUIDANCE: PART (B) QUESTIONS

A01   **A02**

SKILL   ADAPTIVE LEARNING

Question to be answered: Explain two causes of the United Nations' success in helping the transition to a new government in Namibia in 1989.

(8 marks)

1   **Analysis Question 1: What is the question type testing?**
In this question you have to demonstrate that you have knowledge and understanding of the key features and characteristics of the period studied. In this particular case it is knowledge and understanding of the outcomes of UN intervention in Namibia in 1989.

You also have to explain, analyse and make judgements about historical events and periods to explain why something happened.

2   **Analysis Question 2: What do I have to do to answer the question well?**
Obviously you have to write about the UN in Namibia! But it isn't just a case of writing everything you know. You have to write about why the UN was successful in helping achieve the transition to a new Namibian government. To do this well, you need to give the detail showing what the UN did, but you need to make sure you explain why that detail actually led to a successful outcome. We call this explaining why your chosen causes produced the given outcome (i.e. a new Namibian government).

So in this case, there are several causes of the UN being successful in Namibia. You might write about the changing circumstances in southern Africa or the work of the UNTAG, for example.

3   **Analysis Question 3: Are there any techniques I can use to make it very clear that I am doing what is needed to be successful?**
This is an 8-mark question and you need to make sure you leave enough time to answer the other two questions fully (they are worth 22 marks in total). Therefore you need to get straight in to writing your answer. The question asks for two reasons, so it's a good idea to write two paragraphs and to begin each paragraph with phrases like 'One reason was…', 'Another reason was…'. You will get a maximum of 4 marks for each cause you explain, so make sure you give two causes.

How many marks you score for each reason will depend on how well you use accurate and factual information to explain why the clashes occurred.

Answer A

There were two reasons why the United Nations was successful in Namibia. It was becoming less important for the South African government to be involved there and UNTAG successfully managed the elections and transition to a new Namibian government.

What are the strengths and weaknesses of Answer A?

It isn't a very good answer. It has the strength of setting out two reasons, but it hasn't provided factual information to support those reasons, or explained why the United Nations helped the transition to the new Namibian government. It is doubtful that this answer would score more than 2 marks.

Answer B

There were two reasons why the transition to a new Namibian government was successful.

The first reason was that circumstances were changing for South Africa and it was becoming less important for the South African government to be involved there. South Africa operated a system of apartheid in both its own country and Namibia. This had led to fierce criticism around the world and many countries had imposed trade sanctions against South Africa, even though the UN had not made them compulsory. There was also a growing call for reform from white South Africans themselves, partly because of increasing objections to apartheid and partly because of the toll it was taking on their armed forces. It was felt that South African troops would be better used tackling the instability in their own country. So South Africa did not intervene in Namibia, allowing a successful transition.

Another reason why the transition to a new Namibian government was successful was of UNTAG. The UN Transition Assistance Group worked with the UNHCR to ensure that thousands of Namibian refugees returned home and registered to vote in the November elections. The elections went ahead peacefully with a 97 per cent turnout because UNTAG had overseen the disarming of both the SADF (South African Defence Force) and SWAPO (South West Africa Peoples Organisation), the withdrawal of the SADF and demobilisation of SWAPO. UNTAG was well organised throughout Namibia in both local and national centres. From these centres it set up regular meetings to deal with tensions as they arose and was able to prevent South Africa from derailing the elections. So UNTAG created a peaceful environment which allowed successful transition.

What are the strengths and weaknesses of Answer B?

This is an excellent answer. It gives two reasons and provides factual support in showing how those causes brought about the transition to a new Namibian government. It uses terms such as apartheid, UNTAG, SWAPO and SADF correctly without getting distracted by describing or explaining them. Instead, they are written about as part of the reason why the transition was successful. It would be likely to receive full marks.

Challenge a friend

Use the Student Book to set a part (b) question for a friend. Then look at the answer. Does it do the following things?

☐ Provide two causes
☐ Provide detailed information to support the causes
☐ Show how the causes led to the given outcome.

If it does, you can tell your friend that the answer is very good!

5. THE UNITED NATIONS AT BAY, 1990–2011

LEARNING OBJECTIVES

- Understand the key developments in the UN's role 1990–2011
- Explain the problems facing the UN after 1990
- Evaluate how successful the UN was after 1990.

It was hoped that the end of the Cold War would enable the United Nations to be more effective. At first this seemed to be the case, and there were more peacekeeping operations than ever before. The scope of the operations also grew. The UN became more involved in what happened after ceasefires were put in place, as Boutros Boutros-Ghali's 1992 report 'An Agenda for Peace' showed.

In 2000 another report, this time by Kofi Annan, widened the UN's scope still further by suggesting that it ought to intervene wherever human rights were being violated. This came after UN failures in Bosnia and Rwanda, where genocides had taken place. Unfortunately, as events in Sudan were soon to show, the UN would continue to face such problems.

The positive impact of the end of the Cold War proved to be short-lived. International co-operation was no easier as the world entered the new millennium and there was to be no shortage of crises.

5.1 THE UN AND LONG-TERM PEACE

LEARNING OBJECTIVES

- ☐ Understand how the UN developed strategies for achieving long-term peace
- ☐ Understand the key developments in peacekeeping after 1990
- ☐ Evaluate the developments in the UN's work made under Boutros Boutros-Ghali and Kofi Annan.

THE UN FROM 1990

After the Cold War ended in 1991, the work of the United Nations continued to grow. Increasingly it aimed at achieving long-term peace in troubled countries by dealing with the issues that caused the conflicts in the first place. There were three key developments that contributed to this.

- There was an increase in peacekeeping missions, especially for internal conflicts (within a country, civil wars).
- In 1992 Boutros-Ghali produced his report 'An Agenda For Peace'.
- The 'Responsibility to Protect' policy was approved at the UN World Summit in 2005.

The scope of the United Nations' interventions around the world therefore grew considerably.

INCREASE IN MISSIONS

Without the divisions in the Security Council caused by the Cold War, the use of the veto declined. This resulted in 48 peacekeeping missions from 1989 to 2011, compared with 18 from 1946 to 1989. These missions increasingly involved intervening in civil wars, especially where there were human rights abuses involved. Often the UN would stay after a conflict ended to help nations achieve a lasting peace.

BOUTROS-GHALI'S 'AN AGENDA FOR PEACE', 1992

This proposed the idea of **peace building** as well as peacekeeping. Peace building involves dealing with the causes of conflict. Then Secretary-General Boutros-Ghali, suggested that the UN work to:

- disarm fighting factions
- protect human rights
- create and reform political systems and government organisations
- monitor elections
- repatriate refugees
- train security forces.

KEY TERM

peace building securing long-lasting peace by dealing with the causes of a conflict

These ideas were not completely new (see Namibia, pages 83–84) but, after the Cold War, the time seemed right to develop them further and make the UN more effective.1992 was also the year that a separate Department of Peacekeeping Operations (DPKO) was created to manage the UN's work in maintaining international peace and security.

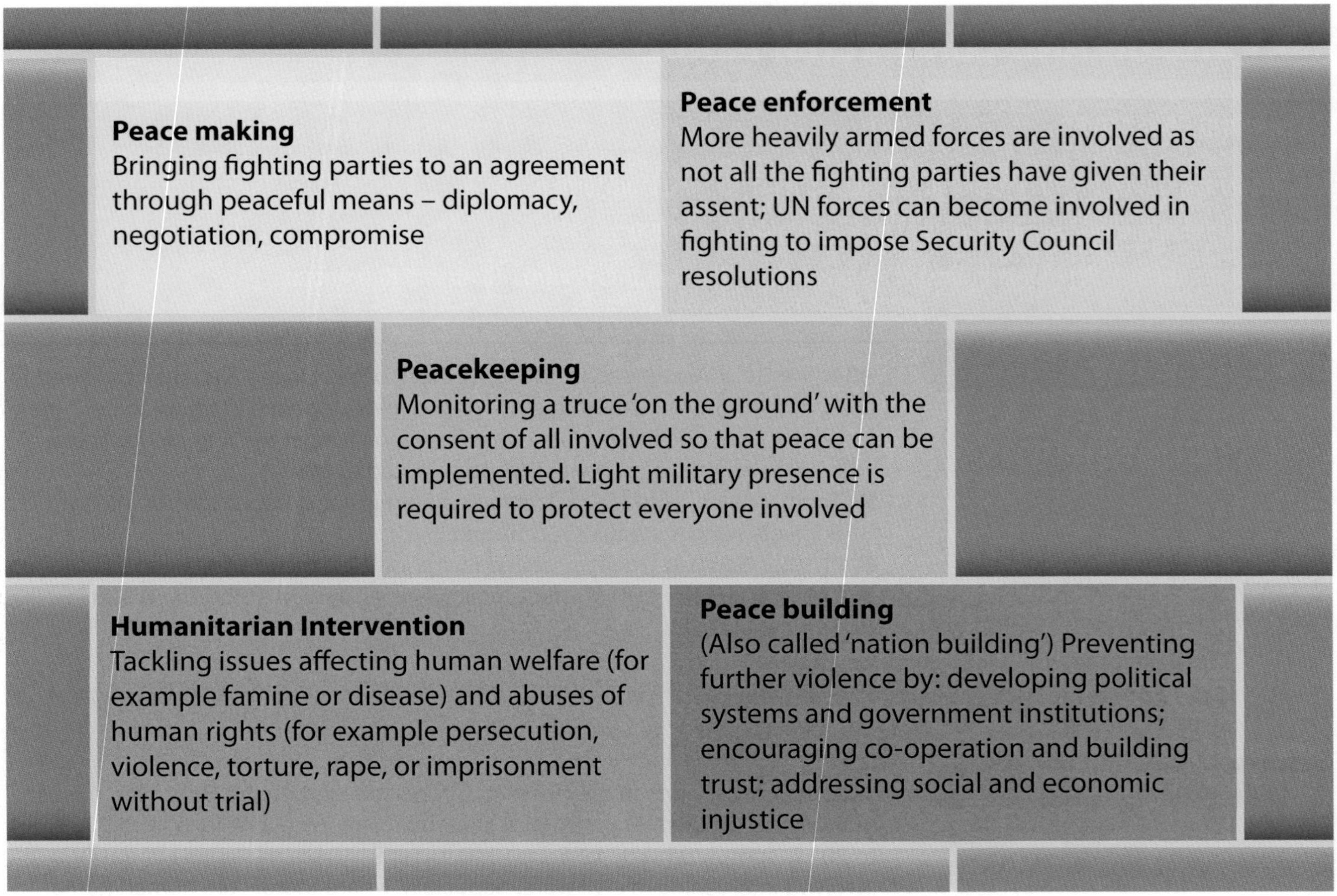

Peace making

Bringing fighting parties to an agreement through peaceful means – diplomacy, negotiation, compromise

Peace enforcement

More heavily armed forces are involved as not all the fighting parties have given their assent; UN forces can become involved in fighting to impose Security Council resolutions

Peacekeeping

Monitoring a truce 'on the ground' with the consent of all involved so that peace can be implemented. Light military presence is required to protect everyone involved

Humanitarian Intervention

Tackling issues affecting human welfare (for example famine or disease) and abuses of human rights (for example persecution, violence, torture, rape, or imprisonment without trial)

Peace building

(Also called 'nation building') Preventing further violence by: developing political systems and government institutions; encouraging co-operation and building trust; addressing social and economic injustice

▲ Figure 5.1 UN missions: building blocks for peace

THE 'RESPONSIBILITY TO PROTECT'

SOURCE A

From the Millennium Report by Kofi Annan in 2000.

If humanitarian intervention is, indeed, an unacceptable assault on a nation's sovereignty, how should we respond... to gross and systematic violations of human rights that offend... our common humanity?

KEY TERMS

war crimes the deliberate killing, torture or inhumane treatment of people that are not militarily necessary

crimes against humanity inhumane acts against civilian populations, especially where specific groups are targeted

The UN believed that conflict often arose from social and economic inequality and a lack of respect for human rights. To achieve long-term peace it was important to tackle these issues wherever conflict occurred.

Two genocides in the 1990s, in Bosnia (see pages 99–103) and in Rwanda, had highlighted the UN's failure to protect ethnic communities. These atrocities led Secretary-General Kofi Annan to challenge the idea that a nation's sovereignty – its right to govern itself without interference – must be respected even if it ignored the human rights of its own people. In 1998, he made an important speech in which he said that the UN had the right to intervene if governments committed human rights abuses on their own people. In 2000 he discussed this proposal again in a special Millennium Report (see Source A).

In 2005 at the UN World Summit, the following 'Responsibility to Protect' principles were agreed.
- Nations are responsible for protecting all their people from genocide/ethnic cleansing, **war crimes** and **crimes against humanity**.
- The international community must encourage and support each other to ensure that these responsibilities are achieved.
- If a country fails to protect all of its people, the international community must take action.

ACTIVITY

1 Briefly explain why the end of the Cold War should have made the UN more effective.
2 What evidence have you come across so far that (a) suggests the UN did become more effective and (b) that it did not?
3 What arguments are there for and against the UN developments outlined in (a) 'Agenda for Peace' (1992) and (b) 'Responsibility to Protect' (2005)?

5.2 THE UN ROLE IN THE GULF WARS

LEARNING OBJECTIVES

- Understand why the UN became involved in the first Gulf War (1991)
- Understand the outcome of the first Gulf War and its impact on the UN
- Understand why the second Gulf War damaged the UN.

THE FIRST GULF WAR, 1991

EXTRACT A

From a recent book on the United Nations.

The turning point for the post-Cold War era occurred in the Council's response to the Iraqi invasion of Kuwait in August 1990. The lack of a UN standing army and the scale of the challenge rendered UN peacekeepers inappropriate to the task – peace first had to be enforced.

Iraq invaded and occupied its neighbour, Kuwait, on 2 August 1990. It was a clear act of aggression by the Iraqi dictator, Saddam Hussein. Within hours the Security Council met and issued Resolution 660, demanding Iraq's immediate withdrawal.

Over the coming months the UN issued more resolutions against Iraq, including severe trade sanctions. There were embargoes on the purchase of Iraqi oil and the sale of arms to Iraq. Saddam Hussein did not withdraw his forces, however. Finally, on 29 November, the Security Council passed Resolution 678. This allowed for member states to attack Iraq if it did not withdraw from Kuwait by 15 January 1991. Iraq did not, and so Operation Desert Storm was launched.

RESOLUTION 678

Operation Desert Storm enforced the UN's resolution for peace and security with troops instead of simply trying to negotiate an end to the occupation of Kuwait. This was allowed by the UN Charter.

As the UN did not have its own forces it relied on member states to provide the necessary troops, resources and funding. It was the US-led forces that directed military operations. The **coalition** included many Arab states, such as Egypt and Syria, as well as nations from every other continent.

OPERATION DESERT STORM, 1991

The first air attack was on 17 January 1991. Ground operations began on 24 February and Iraq accepted all UN resolutions on 28 February. The military operation to enforce Resolution 678 had been quick and successful. As a result, confidence in the UN grew significantly. It became more willing to intervene further in other disputes, including civil wars such as Somalia and Bosnia (see pages 100–103, 104–106).

Kuwait City parade celebrating the defeat of Iraqi forces by Allied troops enforcing UN Resolution 678.

THE SIGNIFICANCE OF THE FIRST GULF WAR FOR THE UN

Reputation

The UN's reputation greatly improved:
- it took swift, decisive action
- the Security Council worked together effectively
- Desert Storm was successful

Methods

The UN *enforced* peace:
- it went beyond the usual method of mediation
- it imposed tough sanctions aimed at forcing Iraq to comply
- Desert Storm was a military operation, approved by the Security Council

Res. 678

Resolution 678 set pattern for future UN military interventions:
- it relied upon willing nations to risk troops and fund operations to enforce UN resolution
- Security Council set out basic aims but left other decisions to military leaders in combat

Res. 688

Resolution 688 broke new ground:
- it saw human rights abuse as threat to *international* peace and security rather than simply a domestic matter

▶ Figure 5.2 Significance of the Gulf War for the UN

FROM GULF WAR 1991 TO GULF WAR 2003

In April 1991, UNIKOM (UN Iraq-Kuwait Observer Mission) was set up. UNIKOM's task was to monitor and protect a demilitarised zone along the Iraq-Kuwait border. It had the power to use force if necessary to ensure Iraq's compliance with its mission. This reflected the new, more confident approach of the UN after the success of Desert Storm.

EXTEND YOUR KNOWLEDGE

UNICEF calculated the number of Iraqi children who died because of sanctions at 500,000. An inadequate diet, contaminated water and limited access to medicine were all problems resulting from sanctions. Rates of cancer and dysentery, for example, increased for the general population but hit children especially hard. Mothers' ability to breastfeed their babies was also affected by sanctions.

EXTEND YOUR KNOWLEDGE

On 11 September 2001 suicide bombers hijacked four passenger planes over the east coast of the USA. Two were flown into the Twin Towers of the World Trade Center in New York; one into the Pentagon; and the hijackers lost control of the fourth, which crashed in Pennsylvania. Over 3,000 people were killed. An Islamist terrorist group, Al-Qaeda was believed to have been responsible. At the time Al-Qaeda was based in Afghanistan, although it also had links with terrorist groups around the world. The USA and Britain invaded Afghanistan before US President Bush turned his attention to Iraq.

The UN took further action against Iraq as it was believed to be a threat to the stability of the Middle East and possibly to world peace. The UN carried out weapons inspections in the 1990s, finding a large number of weapons and technology that were banned under international agreements. It was also thought that Iraq had been developing weapons of mass destruction (WMDs). The Iraqi government tried to interfere with the inspections, although it had been warned not to. The UN therefore imposed harsh economic sanctions.

The sanctions made little difference to the Iraqi government. Instead it was the Iraqi people who suffered. Divisions appeared among the Security Council's permanent five: France and Russia wanted to end sanctions; the USA and Britain refused. The veto meant that there was no solution, although humanitarian measures to supply food and medicine were agreed. They were not enough, however: one estimate has calculated that up to 500,000 Iraqi children died as a result of sanctions.

THE SECOND GULF WAR, 2003

Iraq was the most important issue on the Security Council's agenda again after the terrorist attacks of 11 September 2001. Afterwards, President George W. Bush was determined to fight terrorism – and he included Iraq in his arguments. He asked the UN Security Council to support the use of force to disarm Iraq. Saddam's attitude to disarming, however, meant that using force would probably mean another invasion. If the UN did not give him its backing, Bush made it clear that the USA would go ahead anyway.

Britain agreed with the intelligence shared by the USA. It said Saddam would soon have WMDs, which would destabilise the Middle East. Although Saddam's human rights record was terrible, Britain, the USA and the other nations that invaded Iraq, claimed the invasion was not about regime change. It was to enforce the unanimous resolutions of the UN's Security Council. They included disarming Iraq.

France and Russia vetoed an invasion of Iraq, as did Germany. The USA, Britain and a few other nations (including Australia, Bulgaria, Hungary, Italy, the Netherlands, Poland, Spain and Ukraine) therefore invaded in March 2003

▲ Figure 5.3 US President George W. Bush and the second Gulf War

without Security Council authorisation. The UN could either accept and approve the invasion; or it could condemn it. What it could not do was prevent it. Bush had made the UN irrelevant.

SOURCE C

Protests against British Prime Minister Tony Blair outside No.10 Downing Street. Blair took Britain into the 2003 war against Iraq based on unfounded claims of WMDs.

Saddam was overthrown in April 2003. However, the USA and Britain found the task of dealing with Iraq afterwards too great to manage alone. In May, the Security Council passed a resolution accepting the USA and Britain as occupying powers and, at the request of the Iraqis, appointed a new UN Assistance Mission to Iraq (UNAMI). This time it had a more traditional peacekeeping role and began to help the country rebuild, politically and economically. As of early 2017, it is still there. No evidence of weapons of mass destruction has been found.

THE IMPACT OF THE SECOND GULF WAR ON THE UN

The Gulf War of 2003, and the events in the years before, damaged the reputation of the UN. The UN later declared the 2003 invasion of Iraq as illegal, but it had been unable to take any action to prevent it. The sanctions imposed to make Iraq's government disarm only succeeded in harming the Iraqi people. Unable to stop the USA and Britain from invading Iraq, the UN was accused of weakness. As for the Security Council, it was as divided and impotent as it had been during the Cold War.

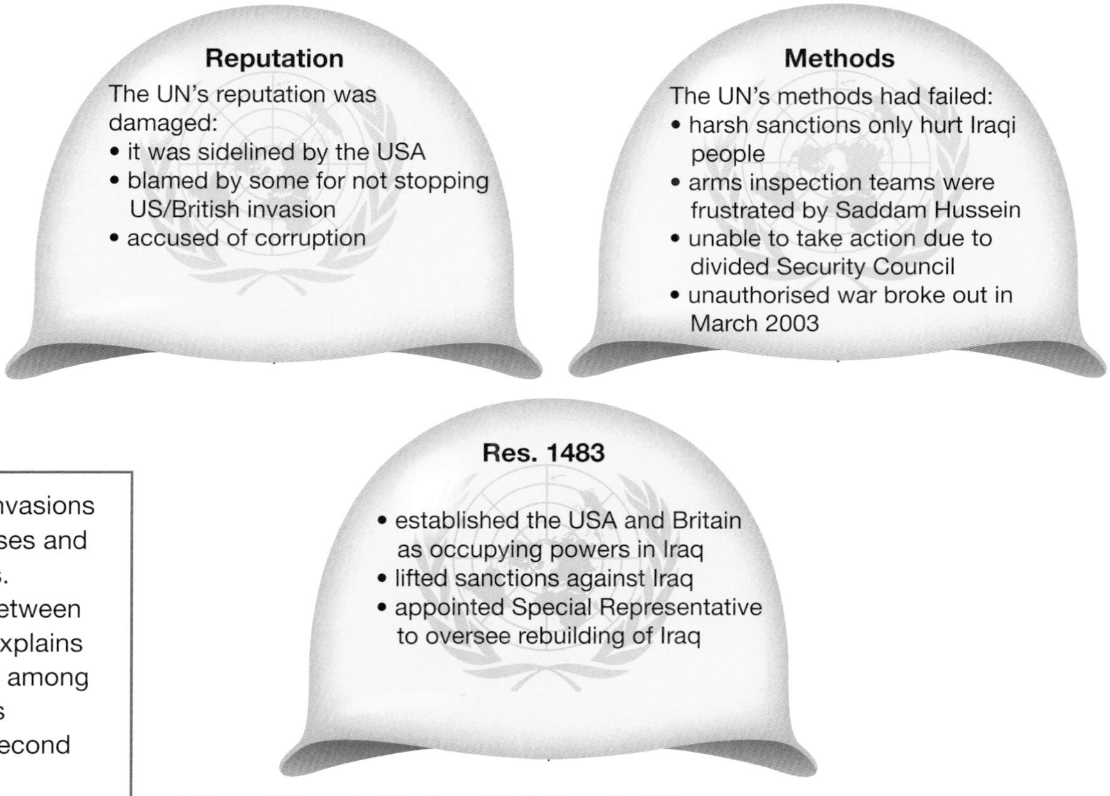

Reputation

The UN's reputation was damaged:
- it was sidelined by the USA
- blamed by some for not stopping US/British invasion
- accused of corruption

Methods

The UN's methods had failed:
- harsh sanctions only hurt Iraqi people
- arms inspection teams were frustrated by Saddam Hussein
- unable to take action due to divided Security Council
- unauthorised war broke out in March 2003

Res. 1483

- established the USA and Britain as occupying powers in Iraq
- lifted sanctions against Iraq
- appointed Special Representative to oversee rebuilding of Iraq

▲ Figure 5.4 Impact of the Second Gulf War on the UN

ACTIVITY

1 For each of the two invasions of Iraq list (a) the causes and (b) the consequences.
2 What had changed between 1991 and 2003 that explains the different attitudes among the Security Council's permanent five to a second invasion of Iraq?

EXAM-STYLE QUESTION

A01 **A02**

Explain **two** ways in which the invasion of Iraq in 2003 was different from that in 1991. **(6 marks)**

HINT

You need to write about both invasions to make a comparison, so make sure you balance your answer between both.

5.3 THE UN IN THE BALKANS: CROATIA, KOSOVO AND BOSNIA, 1991–99

LEARNING OBJECTIVES

- Understand why the UN intervened in the Balkans in 1991–99
- Explain the differences between UN operations in Croatia, Kosovo and Bosnia
- Evaluate the UN's role in Bosnia.

'THEM' AND 'US': WHAT IS AN IDENTITY WAR?

Identity wars can arise when people see themselves as belonging to, or identifying with, an exclusive group of people ('us'), and feel threatened by, or superior to, another group ('them'). A group's identity does not have to be defined by national borders. It can be based on ethnicity, culture, or religion for example. Often one group tries to use power over others, or makes other groups feel threatened.

THE BALKANS

When the Cold War ended with the defeat of communism, nationalism spread through Eastern Europe. During the 1990s the six republics that made up Yugoslavia (which was created after the First World War) broke apart to form independent states as different ethnic groups turned against each other. People looked to their roots to help them determine who they were and where they belonged: they did not see themselves as Yugoslavians but as Serbs, Croats, Bosnians or Slovenians for example.

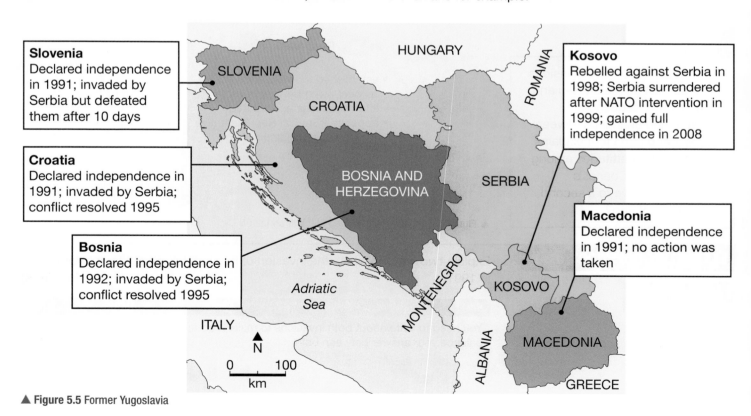

Slovenia
Declared independence in 1991; invaded by Serbia but defeated them after 10 days

Croatia
Declared independence in 1991; invaded by Serbia; conflict resolved 1995

Bosnia
Declared independence in 1992; invaded by Serbia; conflict resolved 1995

Kosovo
Rebelled against Serbia in 1998; Serbia surrendered after NATO intervention in 1999; gained full independence in 2008

Macedonia
Declared independence in 1991; no action was taken

▲ Figure 5.5 Former Yugoslavia

WAR IN CROATIA, 1991–95

In 1990 it became clear that Serbian president Slobodan Milosevic hoped to keep Yugoslavia together under a dominant Serbia. In 1991 Slovenia, Croatia and Macedonia declared independence. Milosevic sent the Yugoslav army into Slovenia but the Slovenians defeated it in 10 days. The Yugoslav army then focused on Croatia, where a large number of Serbs lived. They had not agreed with independence from Yugoslavia. Macedonia, where very few Serbs lived, was ignored.

Concerned about regional security, the European Union held a conference about restoring peace in Yugoslavia. The UN supported it and in January 1992 it sent personnel to help maintain a ceasefire. It then agreed to the creation of UNPROFOR (UN Protective Force). UNPROFOR was to:
- support the humanitarian work of other UN agencies (the UNHCR was involved in helping the thousands of refugees fleeing from the fighting for example)
- monitor the ceasefire and the withdrawal of Yugoslav forces from Croatia
- make sure Croatian government authority was restored in 'pink zones' (see below)
- create UN Protected Areas and make sure that they were demilitarised
- protect civilians and human rights.

This was more traditional peacekeeping, rather than peace enforcement or peace building. It was not an easy task. As 1992 continued:
- UNPROFOR became more involved in protecting civilians
- 'pink zones' remained; these were Serb-dominated areas of Croatia run by the Yugoslav national army
- the demilitarisation was ineffective because in the places the Yugoslav army withdrew from, it left weapons for the Croatian Serbs to use.

The ceasefire broke down in January 1993 when Croatia, impatient with the progress being made, launched an attack against Serb forces, which led to renewed fighting. The ceasefire was only restored through talks run jointly by the UN and European Union.

In 1995 Croatia launched a series of attacks against the Serbs, who by that time were struggling in Bosnia where they had been fighting since 1992. The Croats regained land lost to Serbia and as a result approximately 200,000 Serbs fled Croatia. In November, however, a peace deal was signed in Dayton, Ohio – thanks to US diplomacy, not the UN (see page 102). US Secretary of State, Richard Holbrooke, led the negotiations. The US government wanted minimum UN involvement in Dayton. It did not want news reports of its success damaged by the UN's failures and its unpopularity in the USA.

KOSOVO, 1998–99

Kosovo was a province of Yugoslavia. In 1990 it declared itself an autonomous republic within the Yugoslav federation. When Yugoslavia broke up, however, Kosovo demanded full independence. Serbia did not want this to happen. Slobodan Milosevic had strengthened Serbia's hold on Kosovo in 1989. The Kosovo Liberation Army was formed with the aim of creating an independent Kosovar state. It carried out attacks on Serbian targets until, in 1998, Kosovo rebelled.

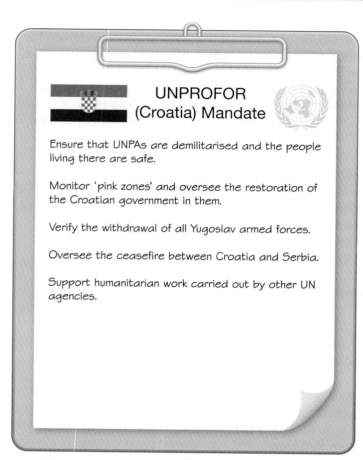

UNPROFOR (Croatia) Mandate

Ensure that UNPAs are demilitarised and the people living there are safe.

Monitor 'pink zones' and oversee the restoration of the Croatian government in them.

Verify the withdrawal of all Yugoslav armed forces.

Oversee the ceasefire between Croatia and Serbia.

Support humanitarian work carried out by other UN agencies.

Many Kosovars were of Albanian origin. The rebellion was triggered by a Serb attack on villages containing mostly ethnic Albanians. Dozens of civilians were killed and thousands more fled as their homes were burned. The USA demanded Serbia withdraw. **NATO** too reacted angrily against Serbian forces attacking civilians.

The situation in Kosovo threatened to destabilise the whole region, and the USA was very concerned. The Security Council could not be relied upon to pass resolutions to defend Kosovo because the USSR was an ally of Serbia and had the veto. NATO took on the role of defending Kosovo instead. In 1999 it launched air attacks against Belgrade after peace negotiations had failed. The attacks lasted 72 days before Milosevic gave in. It was NATO, however, not the UN, that then stepped in to patrol and protect Kosovo.

There were huge human rights issues in Kosovo, including mass **deportations** of Kosovar Albanians into Macedonia, Albania and other neighbouring states. There was great violence and many people were killed, especially the men. After NATO had forced Milosevic's acceptance, the UN set up its Mission in Kosovo (UNMIK).

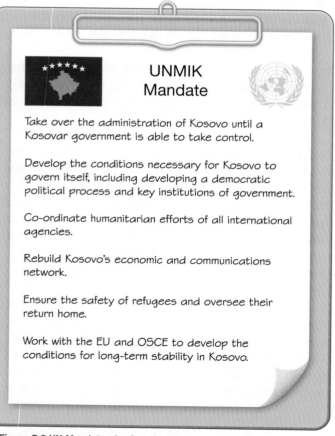

UNMIK Mandate

Take over the administration of Kosovo until a Kosovar government is able to take control.

Develop the conditions necessary for Kosovo to govern itself, including developing a democratic political process and key institutions of government.

Co-ordinate humanitarian efforts of all international agencies.

Rebuild Kosovo's economic and communications network.

Ensure the safety of refugees and oversee their return home.

Work with the EU and OSCE to develop the conditions for long-term stability in Kosovo.

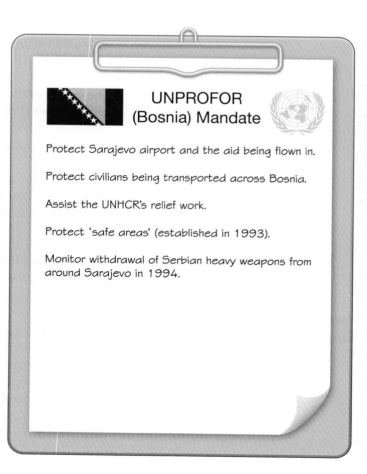

UNPROFOR (Bosnia) Mandate

Protect Sarajevo airport and the aid being flown in.

Protect civilians being transported across Bosnia.

Assist the UNHCR's relief work.

Protect 'safe areas' (established in 1993).

Monitor withdrawal of Serbian heavy weapons from around Sarajevo in 1994.

▲ **Figure 5.6** UN Mandates for Croatia, Kosovo and Bosnia

The UN's approach to Kosovo differed from its approach to Croatia. UNMIK's mandate was unprecedented because it was much more than peacekeeping. The Security Council had given UNMIK enormous, wide-ranging powers over the land, people, government and laws. Its aim was peace *building* to achieve long-term stability in Kosovo by working with the EU and the OSCE.

ACTIVITY

1 Work in pairs. Study the UN response to Croatia. What lessons should the UN have learned from its intervention there?
2 Make a table with two columns and three rows. One column must be headed 'Similarities' and the other 'Differences'. The first row should be labelled 'Croatia', the second 'Kosovo' and the third 'Bosnia'. Complete the first two rows.

BOSNIA, 1991–95

Bosnia was another province of Yugoslavia until 1992. It had a mixed population made up of Bosniaks (Bosnian Muslims), Serbs and Croats. It held a **referendum** on independence from Yugoslavia in 1992. A large majority of Bosniaks and Croats voted in favour. Bosnia was immediately attacked by Bosnian-Serb units of the Yugoslav army. Within 6 weeks large areas were under the control of Serbian commander Ratko Mladić. Sarajevo was besieged by Serb forces and by the end of 1992, the Serbs controlled about 70 per cent of Bosnia.

A policy of ethnic cleansing began. Non-Serbs were sent to prison camps where atrocities took place on a large scale. These included murder, torture, rape, castration and mass executions. The bodies of those killed were usually dumped in common graves. Other crimes against humanity were carried out elsewhere, but the ethnic cleansing of Bosnian Muslims by Serbian forces was by far the worst.

SOURCE D

A family member of one of the victims of the torture camp in Omarska, Western Bosnia, holds a photo of his relative's excavated body during a visit to the site of the camp, 6 August 2006.

THE UN IN BOSNIA

January 1992 UNPROFOR is created
October 1992 UN establishes No-Fly Zones over Bosnia; there is no strategy for enforcing them, however

February 1994 NATO jets shoot down four Serb fighter jets
Serbians bomb Sarajevo market, killing 68 and injuring 200
April 1994 More NATO airstrikes against Serbian targets
July 1994 Serbs cut off Sarajevo and take UN hostages
August 1994 Serbians bomb Sarajevo market again, killing 37 and injuring 90
September 1994 NATO demands Serbs withdraw all their forces from around Sarajevo
November 1994 NATO undertakes more bombing raids on Serbian targets in Bosnia; Serbs take UN hostages

March 1993 the Security Council agrees NATO jets can shoot down any aircraft flying over Bosnia without UN approval
April 1993 UN establishes safe areas policy, starting with Srebrenica
June 1993 UN declares Sarajevo, Bihać, Tuzla, Zepa and Gorazde as safe areas

March 1995 UN releases figures showing 4,217 violations of the No-Fly Zones by all sides
May 1995 Serbs take 400 UN hostages as NATO bombs Serbian targets
July 1995 Serbs invade safe area of Srebrenica, resulting in the massacre of 7,000 men and boys; hundreds of women are raped
NATO decides that any further attacks on UN safe areas will lead to immediate air strikes, without waiting for UN approval
August 1995 Serbs attack Sarajevo market again; NATO begins 2 weeks of attacks on Serbian targets
September 1995 A lasting ceasefire is negotiated by US Secretary of State Holbrooke
November 1995 Peace conference at Dayton, Ohio, leads to peace agreement in December; the UN plays only a small part in these events

UNPROFOR

In June 1992, the UN sent a peacekeeping protection force (UNPROFOR) into Bosnia. UNPROFOR was already working in Croatia, which had also declared independence. Its tasks were to:

- protect Sarajevo airport and convoys of food and medicine being flown in
- protect convoys of civilians being transported across Bosnia by the International Red Cross
- assist the UNHCR to deliver humanitarian relief throughout Bosnia.

The peacekeepers were allowed to shoot past (rather than at) Serbs trying to block food convoys. This tactic was not successful. UN personnel therefore usually had to plead with Serb forces to let the convoys through. The result was that Serbian forces saw the UN as weak.

The UN's image was weakened even more by its other peacekeeping efforts in Bosnia.

NO-FLY ZONES AND SAFE AREAS

In October 1992, the Security Council declared no-fly zones over Bosnia. Although NATO jet fighters had permission to shoot down unauthorised aircraft, they first needed UN approval. However, the UN did not want to give permission as it wanted to avoid doing anything that might anger Serbian forces and lead them to attack peacekeepers and humanitarian workers. This meant that the no-fly zones were ineffective.

SOURCE E

UNPROFOR soldiers in Sarajevo.

In 1993 the UN created **safe areas** in Bosnia after thousands of Muslims, who were escaping ethnic cleansing, fled to the town of Srebrenica, doubling its population. Serb attacks on Srebrenica prevented the UN from delivering desperately needed food supplies. The Security Council tried a new approach: it declared Srebrenica a 'safe area', meaning it was protected from attack, and sent a small group of peacekeepers. Five more safe areas were created, including Sarajevo, Bosnia's capital.

The new safe areas had mixed results, mostly bad.
- Over 30,000 peacekeepers were required, but the Security Council only agreed to 7,600. UN member countries were unwilling to send troops and so only 5,000 were provided.
- The Bosnian government used safe areas as bases from which to attack Serbs, who then attacked Bosnian targets.
- Shelling and sniper attacks on Sarajevo continued.
- Living conditions were terrible: overcrowding, unemployment and crime were big problems.
- But, there was less violence, fewer casualties and more humanitarian support in safe areas.

A CHANGE IN TACTICS: 1994–95

Labelling certain places 'safe areas' was not enough to protect them. One attack on Sarajevo market killed 68 and injured 200. The UN then agreed that NATO air strikes could be used against Serbian targets. Rather than stopping the Serbs, they changed tactics.

In 1994 the Serbs threatened the safe area of Bihać. NATO bombed Serbian airbases and military sites in Bosnia to warn them against attacking the town, so the Serbs took 400 UN hostages. This was a change in Serbian tactics. The UN became more cautious about putting its people in situations where they might be taken hostage. This made the peacekeeping task even more difficult.

SOURCE F

The UN Commissioner for Human Rights, Zeid Ra'ad Al Hussein, explains what went wrong in Srebrenica.

'Mr. Zeid [spoke] of what he termed the UN's "clumsy" efforts in addressing the growing threats on the ground during the early days of the Bosnian conflict. From wavering displays of authority to a non-committal use of force in countering an increasingly scaled-up Bosnian Serb aggression against ethnic minorities, [he] described the Organization's "hesitation" and "timidity" as being key to the Srebrenica tragedy.

"We got it wrong, so wrong, although the people of Srebrenica knew full well who they were confronted with and what was in store for them," he stated.'

THE SREBRENICA MASSACRE

In July 1995, Bosnian Serbs invaded the 'safe area' of Srebrenica. They took 30 peacekeepers hostage and threatened to attack a UN compound where thousands of refugees were sheltered.

The Bosnian Serb commander, Ratko Mladić, agreed to allow Srebrenica's Muslims to leave safely. Women and children were to be sent out first. Once the men and boys were separated, however, they were executed: 7,000 in total. When the women and children were sent out, many young women were pulled off the buses and raped.

THE OUTCOME OF THE BOSNIAN WAR

After the Srebrenica massacre, NATO decided that any further Serbian attacks would immediately result in air strikes against them, without waiting for UN approval. Another attack on Sarajevo market led to 2 weeks of NATO attacks. The UN had removed all peacekeepers from surrounding areas so that the Serbs could not take hostages. The Serbs were also attacked by the Croatians.

Finally the Serbs were ready to negotiate. The Dayton Peace Accords, dividing Bosnia into two (51 per cent for Bosnian Croats and Muslims and 49 per cent for Bosnian Serbs) were overseen by, and signed in, the USA. However, the image of the UN in America was very damaged and the US government did not want it to play any major role in Dayton.

The failure of the UN to protect the population of the 'safe' area of Srebrenica did great damage to the UN's reputation. It was one reason why the USA did not want the UN to have a role in the Dayton Accords (see page 101). The memory of the Srebrenica massacre, and the lessons to learn from it, still overshadow the UN's recent history (see Source F).

Serbs not concerned by international condemnation

Use of UN peacekeepers as hostages: UN vulnerable

Lack of armed forces / commitment from the USA and Europe

The UN at bay: Bosnia 1992–95

UN inadequate enforcement of policies

Feared retaliation; needed ALL to co-operate for humanitarian efforts

▲ Figure 5.7 Bosnia: why did UNPROFOR not succeed?

▼ Bosnia: outcomes for the UN

▽ EVIDENCE OF SUCCESS	▽ EVIDENCE OF FAILURE
No-fly zones and safe areas did save some lives	No-fly zones and safe areas were frequently violated
Over 2.7 million Bosnians received humanitarian aid	UN peacekeepers were taken hostage, limiting the UN's ability to act
When the UN finally allowed NATO air strikes against the Serbs, the Serbs agreed to negotiate peace	There were not enough UN peacekeepers to carry out all its policies
UN peacekeepers protected access to Sarajevo airport for humanitarian and peacekeeping efforts	Relations between the UN and the USA were bad (Dayton Accords, for example)
	The image of the UN was severely damaged, especially by the Srebrenica massacre; it appeared weak and was unable to end the conflict
	Lack of support for UN peacekeeping from international governments
	Progress relied on NATO and the USA

WAR CRIMES IN THE BALKANS

In 1993, the UN created the International Criminal Tribunal for the Former Yugoslavia. Crimes such as starvation, rape and torture in Serbian prison camps had been well advertised by the international media. Evidence of ethnic cleansing was found too. The first trial began on 7 May 1996. A total of one 161 people were indicted for war crimes committed in the Balkans between 1991 and 2001.

ACTIVITY

1 Complete the row on Bosnia in the table you started on the similarities and differences between Croatia, Kosovo and Bosnia.
2 Why might the conflicts in Croatia, Kosovo and Bosnia be described as an identity war rather than simply a civil war?
3 You are a UN official writing a report on UNPROFOR's activities in Bosnia. You must evaluate the UN's performance. What were the UN's aims? What did UNPROFOR achieve? What failed and why? What lessons should the UN learn from events in Bosnia? You may present your information however you wish. You might want to research some pictures or maps. Your report could be broken down as follows.
  ■ UNPROFOR's aims and role in Bosnia
  ■ What worked?
  ■ Mistakes made – what were they?
  ■ If another such situation arose, what should the UN do differently?

EXAM-STYLE QUESTION

A01   **A02**

SKILL ▶ ADAPTIVE LEARNING

Explain **two** causes of the weak response of the UN to the Bosnian crisis.   **(8 marks)**

HINT

Make sure you look at two reasons and explain how they made the UN's response look weak. Don't just give reasons.

5.4 THE UN IN AFRICA: SOMALIA, MOZAMBIQUE AND SUDAN

LEARNING OBJECTIVES

Understand why and how the UN was involved in Somalia, Mozambique and Sudan

Explain why the UN failed in Somalia, but succeeded in Mozambique

Understand how events in Sudan harmed the reputation of the UN.

THE UN IN SOMALIA, 1991–95

The Somali people are divided into different clans. The clan is an important part of a Somali's identity. These clans became involved in a violent power struggle, resulting in the overthrow of an unpopular government. It also led to civil war breaking out in Somalia in January 1991.

The civil war led to the breakdown of law, order and government throughout the country as different warlords seized control of whatever land they could and then fought each other. The two most important warlords were Generals Aideed and Ali Mahdi. The war was made worse by crop failure and famine. Crops and cattle became targets of looters and militias, while workers trying to distribute aid were robbed and terrorised.

UNOSOM AND UNITAF

In March 1992 talks at UN headquarters in Geneva led to a ceasefire in Somalia. In April 1992 the Security Council agreed to a multinational peacekeeping mission to Somalia, known as UNOSOM. In September, 500 UN peacekeepers arrived but made little difference. Several warlords did not agree with the UN being in Somalia, and the looting and violence continued.

As the humanitarian crisis in Somalia worsened, the Security Council agreed to send a new Unified Task Force (UNITAF) to create safe conditions for the delivery of humanitarian aid. It was made up of 25,400 US troops plus 12,900 troops from other member states and arrived in January 1993. Other UN organisations working in Somalia included the FAO, UNICEF, the UNHCR and the WHO. The International Red Cross was one of many other groups helping relief efforts.

SOURCE G

French and US troops protect UNICEF from attempts to disrupt food distribution in Mogadishu.

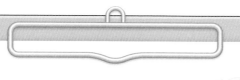

UNOSOM I (Apr. 1992)
- monitor ceasefire in Mogadishu
- protect UN personnel, equipment and supplies, and escort supplies to where they are needed

UNITAF (Dec. 1992)
- establish a safe environment for the delivery of humanitarian assistance
- work with UNOSOM I to secure important towns and villages and to ensure distribution of humanitarian aid
- restore peace, stability, law and order

UNOSOM II (May 1993)
Its mandate was under Chapter VII of the UN Charter, allowing it to take enforcement action if necessary. UNOSOM II was to continue the mandate of UNITAF and:
- enable national reconciliation
- disarm the warlords
- help the Somali people to rebuild a national government based on democracy
- contribute towards the repair of Somalia's economy

▲ Figure 5.8 The UN's mandates in Somalia from UNOSOM I to UNOSOM II via UNITAF

HAD THE UN SUCCEEDED BY MAY 1993?
- UNITAF enabled food and medicine to be distributed to the Somali people so that within a few months the famine was ending.
- There was an uneasy truce between the warlords.
- Violence had stopped where there were UN troops, who covered about 40 per cent of Somalia.
- In some places, armed militia members fled to the countryside resulting in banditry.

There were not yet the conditions to build long-term peace, however. Firstly, there was no effective government or police force in Somalia. Boutros-Ghali believed disarming the warlords was a top priority for long-term stability, but trying to do this could put UN workers in danger.

In May 1993, a new mission, UNOSOM II, was created. It continued the work begun by UNOSOM I and UNITAF by encouraging disarmament and reconciliation. It also had a mandate to:
- enforce UN resolutions if necessary
- restore peace, law and order
- help the Somalis to rebuild their nation.

This was the first time since the Congo in the 1960s that the UN had directly intervened in a state's own internal affairs, and it was the first time it had done so with the agreement of the Security Council.

UNOSOM II

EXTEND YOUR KNOWLEDGE

On 3 October 1993, an American Special Forces unit went on a secret mission to hunt down General Aideed. The mission failed. Two US helicopters were shot down, 18 American troops were killed and dozens of others were wounded and trapped around Mogadishu. UN peacekeeping troops had to rescue them. Dead American soldiers were shown on television being dragged through the streets, naked. This story of this operation is told in the film *Black Hawk Down*.

Warlord General Aideed saw disarmament as a means of weakening him and began attacking the UN. One attack, on 5 June 1993, killed 24 UN troops. The Security Council passed an unprecedented, unanimous resolution: all necessary measures were to be taken against anyone carrying out, or encouraging, attacks against the UN. US Special Forces were involved and there was a US$25,000 reward for Aideed's capture.

The UN was unable to solve the problems in Somalia. Violence and looting continued despite over US$2.5 million a day being spent on the war. On 31 March 1994 the USA withdrew its troops, greatly weakening the operation. In November 1994, the Security Council agreed to withdraw from Somalia by 31 March 1995.

By the time the UN left Somalia, the warlords were still very much opposed to each other. Although there was no longer any famine, the lack of political stability meant that the UN's intervention in Somalia was, overall, a failure. It was unable to fulfil its long-term aims of restoring law and order and helping Somalis to rebuild their country.

WHY DID THE UN FAIL TO FIND A POLITICAL SOLUTION IN SOMALIA?

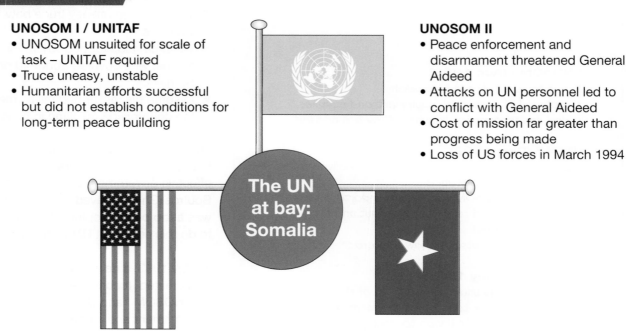

UNOSOM I / UNITAF
- UNOSOM unsuited for scale of task – UNITAF required
- Truce uneasy, unstable
- Humanitarian efforts successful but did not establish conditions for long-term peace building

UNOSOM II
- Peace enforcement and disarmament threatened General Aideed
- Attacks on UN personnel led to conflict with General Aideed
- Cost of mission far greater than progress being made
- Loss of US forces in March 1994

The UN at bay: Somalia

USA
- Commitment dwindled with UNOSOM II
- Somalia failing and very unpopular with American public opinion
- USA withdrew troops in March 1994

Somalia
- Nature of the conflict: competing warlords, militia mingled with civilians
- Aideed and Mahdi not reconciled
- Lack of government, centrally and locally
- Fractured clan-based conflict

▲ Figure 5.9 Why the UN failed, politically, in Somalia

EXAM-STYLE QUESTION

A01   A02

SKILL ADAPTIVE LEARNING

Explain **two** causes of the UN's failure in Somalia.   **(8 marks)**

HINT

Remember that the focus of the question is the UN. Do not get distracted by describing the problems in Somalia.

ACTIVITY

1. Make a timeline of events in Somalia. Identify successes and setbacks for the UN.
2. Pick what you consider to be the greatest success and biggest setback. Write a couple of sentences explaining your choices.
3. In pairs, decide how far UN intervention in Somalia was a failure. You should use your answers to questions 1 and 2 to help you. You should show your final decision on a value continuum and write a short paragraph underneath explaining how you came to your answer.

THE UN IN MOZAMBIQUE, 1990–94

ONUMOZ Mandate
Assist in implementation of GPA and:

1. Military Situation
• monitor ceasefire
• separate and demobilise fighting forces, including private militias
• monitor withdrawal of foreign forces
• secure key transport routes
• provide security for UN and other international agencies

2. Humanitarian Assistance
• protect, co-ordinate and monitor humanitarian assistance
• support and repatriate 1.3 million refugees
• resettle and restore communities

3. Political Support
• advise on, organise and monitor, elections

A civil war had begun in Mozambique not long after it had gained independence from Portugal in 1975. Government forces, led by the Mozambican Liberation Front, fought the South African backed Mozambique Resistance Movement (RENAMO). By 1991, when Mozambique had a severe drought, its economy was badly damaged and its government was under huge strain. Mozambique's people tried to escape both the war and hunger.

By October 1992 both sides in the civil war were exhausted and signed the General Peace Agreement (GPA). The agreement included asking the UN to send in a peacekeeping force. In December 1992, the Security Council created ONUMOZ, the UN mission for Mozambique. Its wide-ranging mandate combined humanitarian, peacekeeping and political tasks.

◀ **Figure 5.10** UN mandate for ONUMOZ

ONUMOZ IN ACTION

The mandate for ONUMOZ was designed to deal with key threats to the GPA and build long-term peace and stability. If the drought and violence could be dealt with, ONUMOZ might succeed. If not:
■ without humanitarian relief, conflict over limited resources would continue
■ without the ceasefire, and the demobilising and disarming of various militia groups, humanitarian aid would not reach the people
■ without settling the political situation, confidence in the GPA would be lost
■ without achieving the points above, there would be little possibility of peaceful elections.

UN Special Representative Aldo Ajello led ONUMOZ. He was given more authority than usual to make decisions. This authority meant he could deal with problems quickly, without having to ask the Security Council, so Mozambicans had more confidence in the whole process.

One key method of giving Mozambicans more confidence in the UN and the GPA was using a large UNCIVPOL force. All parties involved had agreed to this. UNCIVPOL monitored all police activities, including those of private security firms. It worked with, and supported, the Mozambique police. Its role included ensuring civil and political rights were respected and overseeing the election campaign, beginning with voter registration.

Mozambique's first multi-party elections were held in October 1994 and were won by the Mozambican Liberation Front. UN forces finally withdrew as planned when their mandate ended in January 1995.

WHY DID ONUMOZ SUCCEED?

Given the outcomes of UN missions in Somalia and Bosnia, why was Mozambique a success? Probably because key conditions of successful peacekeeping operations were present.

- Everyone involved agreed to the UN intervention – the GPA had already been signed and both sides knew that they were not going to achieve a military victory.
- All major powers (especially the USA), and the Security Council, fully supported ONUMOZ.
- Mozambique was ready to work for peace after so many years of war.

Peace was also helped by changes in South Africa which made it much less of a threat to Mozambique (see Chapter 4), in turn reducing the level of armed conflict there.

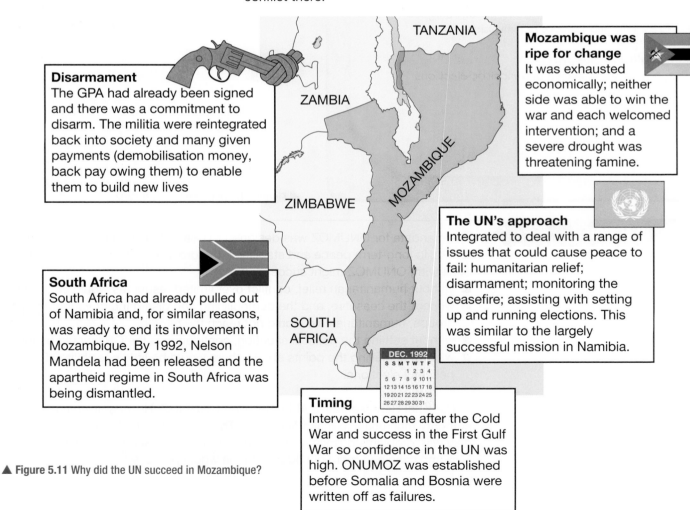

Disarmament
The GPA had already been signed and there was a commitment to disarm. The militia were reintegrated back into society and many given payments (demobilisation money, back pay owing them) to enable them to build new lives

Mozambique was ripe for change
It was exhausted economically; neither side was able to win the war and each welcomed intervention; and a severe drought was threatening famine.

The UN's approach
Integrated to deal with a range of issues that could cause peace to fail: humanitarian relief; disarmament; monitoring the ceasefire; assisting with setting up and running elections. This was similar to the largely successful mission in Namibia.

South Africa
South Africa had already pulled out of Namibia and, for similar reasons, was ready to end its involvement in Mozambique. By 1992, Nelson Mandela had been released and the apartheid regime in South Africa was being dismantled.

Timing
Intervention came after the Cold War and success in the First Gulf War so confidence in the UN was high. ONUMOZ was established before Somalia and Bosnia were written off as failures.

▲ Figure 5.11 Why did the UN succeed in Mozambique?

ACTIVITY

1 Group work and discussion. In small groups, make a table that compares Bosnia, Somalia and Mozambique. You will need to show: causes; what intervention was taken by the UN; consequences.
2 Once this is done, see if you can work out:
   ■ what similarities and differences there were between Somalia and Bosnia
   ■ why Mozambique was more successful than Bosnia and Somalia
   ■ would what was done for Mozambique have worked in Bosnia and / or Somalia?

KEY TERM

Janjaweed originally meaning nomadic Arab tribespeople, it came to mean a violent Arab militia used by the Sudanese government; the Janjaweed was known for its cruel treatment of the people of Darfur

THE UN IN SUDAN, 2005–11

For Sudan, 2005 was an important year. Southern Sudan had been fighting for independence from the north and after years of civil war a truce, called the Comprehensive Peace Agreement, was signed. The United Nations established its mission to Sudan, UNMIS, to help carry out this agreement. It also established an arms embargo on Sudan.

DARFUR AND THE JANJAWEED

EXTEND YOUR KNOWLEDGE

Darfur is populated by dozens of tribes of African farmers and also nomadic Arab herders. As the region has suffered from a lack of water and from pasture becoming very limited, the people have competed for decreasing resources. Traditionally, disputes in Darfur were taken to local councils. The councils were respected but had been abolished by the Sudanese government. This meant that there was no local means of settling conflicts peacefully.

In 2003, while peace negotiations between north and south Sudan were taking place, another crisis developed in the western province of Darfur. Long-term drought had led to tension between Arab nomadic herders and African farming communities, leading to violent conflict. Darfur accused the Sudanese government of neglecting it. Eventually, fighting broke out between Darfur rebel groups and Sudanese government forces, which were allied with the **Janjaweed** militia.

After air attacks on civilian settlements by Sudanese government forces, the Janjaweed would often ride in on horseback, killing the men and raping, kidnapping and murdering women and children. Hundreds of thousands were killed; hundreds of thousands more became refugees. The scale of the atrocities led to events in Darfur being categorised as ethnic cleansing.

DARFUR AND THE INTERNATIONAL COMMUNITY

The African Union (AU) sent a mission, known as AMIS (African Union Mission in Sudan), to Darfur in 2005. In 2006 it helped to negotiate a peace agreement. It was supported by the UN but not by most of the fighting forces in Darfur. Fighting continued and the humanitarian crisis worsened.

Although the Secretary-General of the UN had concerns about Darfur in 2003, the Security Council had not been enthusiastic about intervening before 2006 for several reasons.
■ The peace deal between north and south Sudan was close and they did not want to endanger it.
■ The USA and Britain were fighting in, and occupying, Iraq and did not want to intervene elsewhere.
■ China had just done a deal for Sudanese oil that was important for its rapidly growing economy.
■ Darfur was complicated: different rebel groups were fighting each other as well as the government.

In August 2006, however, the UN wanted to extend its mission to Darfur. The Sudanese government would not allow it. The UN instead helped to support AMIS while developing plans for a joint UN / AU mission.

A FAILURE TO PROTECT?

In 2007 the UN sent 19,000 peacekeepers to Darfur. Although the UN World Summit of 2005 agreed a set of principles in 'Responsibility to Protect', they were allowed to defend themselves and protect any civilians that they could, but that was all. The UN peacekeepers were told that their mission was to:

- monitor events
- protect humanitarian relief efforts
- support voluntary disarmament.

An ex-Secretary General of the UN, Kofi Annan, spoke out saying that it was not enough. He said that force was necessary to protect human rights and lives in Sudan.

UNAMID

In 2008 UNAMID, the joint AU / UN mission, sent 18,000 peacekeepers and police to Sudan. This kind of joint operation was unusual for the UN. Although the UN had used NATO in the Balkans, for example, its work with the AU was more of a partnership. Despite combining efforts in this way, progress was slow. There were still different rebel groups fighting each other as well as the government, and the humanitarian crisis continued to get worse.

By 2009 there were 16,370 aid workers from a variety of international organisations helping 4.7 million people in Darfur. After March 2009 the number of aid workers was reduced quickly as Sudan forced several international organisations to leave. Its leader, Omar al-Bashir, did this after the International Criminal Court (ICC) called for him to be arrested on charges of war crimes. UNAMID, which stayed in Sudan, was overworked, under-resourced and often unable to protect civilians.

UNAMID Mandate

- protect civilians, without prejudice

- help the delivery of humanitarian aid by UN and other international agencies

- protect aid and humanitarian workers

- mediate between the government of Sudan and armed groups that have not signed the 2006 Darfur peace agreement

- work to help address conflict in communities, including the root causes of the conflict

- assist in promoting human rights, the rule of law and political processes

- monitor Sudan's borders with Chad and the Central African Republic

◀ Figure 5.12 UNAMID mandate

2008 Rebel groups launch a major attack against the important Darfur city of Omdurman

2010 Fighting escalates in Darfur causing tens of thousands to flee their homes. The ICC issues another arrest warrant for al-Bashir, this time for genocide. A ceasefire deal is signed but doesn't last due to the conflict between rebel groups

March 2009 The ICC issues arrest warrants for President al-Bashir. The Sudanese government forces 16 agencies working in Sudan (including three in Darfur) to leave

July 2011 Rebel groups forming the LJM sign a peace agreement. Some others fight on

SUDAN, 2011

ACTIVITY

1 Why could what happened in Sudan be seen as an identity war? What other factors led to the problems in Sudan?

2 In pairs, identify the obstacles faced by the UN in Sudan. Which were they able to overcome? How? Was there anything that the UN could have done differently in the Sudan? If so, what? If not, why not?

SOUTH SUDAN

After the end of the civil war between north and south Sudan a new, independent state of South Sudan was born in 2011. The UN created a mission to help with nation building and developing the conditions necessary for long-term peace and stability. This included providing **military liaison officers** to establish law and order, prevent more conflict, and improve security for South Sudan. It has not been successful, however, and South Sudan is still very unstable. As of early 2017, the UN is still in there.

DARFUR

In 2011 the Sudanese government signed a peace agreement with a range of rebel groups, who together formed the Liberation and Justice Movement (LJM). The Liberation and Justice Movement was given an important role in the government of Darfur, including carrying out the peace agreement. Other rebel groups refused to accept it, however, and periods of violence have continued. UNAMID has stayed in Sudan and the refugee camps have become permanent.

EXAM-STYLE QUESTION

A01   **A02**

SKILLS PROBLEM SOLVING, REASONING, DECISION MAKING

How far did the role of the UN in Africa change between 1960 and 2011?

You may use the following in your answer:
■ humanitarian relief agencies
■ enforcing peace.
You **must** also use information of your own.   **(16 marks)**

HINT

Remember that this is about how the role of the UN changed, rather than its successes or failures.

A complex situation on too big a scale?
- There were numerous rebel groups fighting each other as well as the Sudanese government.

- There was the peace agreement to end the north-south Sudanese civil war to deal with first. It could save more lives than intervention in Darfur.

- The USA and Britain had their resources tied up in Iraq.

- The UN did what it could, given the lack of co-operation of Sudan. It even joined forces with the AU to form UNAMID.

Failure to protect?
- There was no mandate to enforce. The intervention, when it came, was not forceful enough.

- The 2005 Basic Principles were ignored and arrest warrants against al-Bashir were not enforced.

The UN could only do what the Sudanese government allowed
- Sudan did not welcome foreign intervention in its dealings with its own rebels. It did allow the UN to work with the AU. It did not allow the UN to extend its mission in Sudan to Darfur.

- Sudan allowed the UN mission to Sudan to help implement the peace with South Sudan until 2011.

- The issuing of arrest warrants by the ICC for President al-Bashir led to him expelling 16 international organisations. This stretched UNAMID's resources.

▲ **Figure 5.13** Overview of the UN in Sudan, 2005–11

CONCLUSION

The League of Nations was created after the First World War and did not survive the Second World War. The very fact that the Second World War broke out means that it did not, ultimately, succeed in its aims, but this does not decrease its significance. Its successor, the United Nations, was developed using some of the lessons learned from the League's weaknesses and mistakes.

The UN too has had mixed success. As Source F shows, the UN continues trying to learn from its own mistakes too. Much of its continuing humanitarian work, through organisations such as UNICEF, the UNHCR and WHO, is not advertised unless there is a large-scale tragedy. The world's nations put their own interests first, however, which is a problem when it comes to collective security. Nevertheless, many UN peacekeepers have been injured or killed in carrying out their duties.

The ideals and beliefs that led to the League being founded, however, are at least as relevant now as in 1919. And studying the history of international co-operation has, perhaps, never been as important.

RECAP

RECALL QUIZ

1 How is peace building different from peacekeeping?
2 What important development in the UN's role was agreed at the UN World Summit in 2005?
3 Give the years of the two Gulf Wars.
4 Which world leader started the second Gulf War? Give the name (including middle initial) and nation.
5 In which conflict did the Srebrenica Massacre occur?
6 Who bombed Serbia into complying over Bosnia and Kosovo?
7 Name a Somali warlord.
8 By what name was the Mozambique Resistance Movement better known?
9 What was the name of the violent militia in Darfur?
10 Which new country was created in 2011?

CHECKPOINT

STRENGTHEN

S1 Which permanent members of the Security Council vetoed a second invasion of Iraq?
S2 What was the name of the country to which Slovenia, Bosnia, Serbia, Croatia and Kosovo all once belonged?
S3 Which UN intervention in Africa was successful?

CHALLENGE

C1 What is the difference between an identity war and a civil war?
C2 Give two reasons why the UN's intervention in Somalia was so difficult.
C3 Give two occasions between 1990 and 2011 when the UN's lack of its own armed forces proved to be a weakness.

SUMMARY

- The UN widened the scope of its interventions after the Cold War.
- The UN did not authorise the second Gulf War.
- Identity wars have spread since 1990.
- The breakdown of Yugoslavia involved the UN in Croatia, Bosnia and Kosovo.
- The UN has worked with other international agencies, such as NATO and the EU in enforcing and building peace.
- The Security Council veto still caused some problems after the Cold War.
- Drought and famine made the problems in Somalia and Sudan much worse.
- Mozambique was an overall success for the UN.
- Humanitarian work has often proved more successful for the UN than peace building and work with political aims.
- There has been an increase in the numbers of people indicted for war crimes since 1990.

EXAM GUIDANCE: PART (C) QUESTIONS

A01   **A02**

SKILLS   PROBLEM SOLVING, REASONING, DECISION MAKING

Question to be answered: How far did the United Nations' role in promoting human rights change in the years 1991 to 2011?

You may use the following in your answer:
- the Bosnian conflict 1991–95
- Sudan 2005–11.

You **must** also use information of your own.   **(16 marks)**

1   **Analysis Question 1: What is the question type testing?**

In this question you have to demonstrate that you have knowledge and understanding of the key features and characteristics of the period studied. In this particular case it is knowledge and understanding of the changing role of the United Nations in the period 1991–2011 in promoting human rights.

You also have to explain, analyse and make judgements about historical events and periods to give an explanation and reach a judgement on how far there was change.

2   **Analysis Question 2: What do I have to do to answer the question well?**

You have been given two factors on which to write: you don't have to use those factors (though it might be wise to do so). You must, however, include at least one factor, other than those you have been given. But you must avoid just giving the information. What changes in the UN's role in promoting human rights do they show?

You are also asked 'how far' the UN's role in promoting human rights changed. So when discussing these events you need to consider what changed and what stayed the same. A part of considering how far the UN's role in promoting human rights changed is to look at other examples. You will see that the question says you must use information of your own. So that should include at least one example other than those you have been given. That example might be Mozambique, Somalia or the Gulf Wars.

3   **Analysis Question 3: Are there any techniques I can use to make it very clear that I am doing what is needed to be successful?**

This is a 16-mark question and you need to make sure you give a substantial answer. You will be up against time pressures so here are some useful techniques to help you succeed.
- Don't write a lengthy introduction. Give a brief introduction that answers the question straight away and shows what your paragraphs are going to be about (you will need to have planned first). You could briefly define peacekeeping.
- To make sure you stay focused on the question and avoid just writing narrative, try to use the words of the question at the beginning of each paragraph.

Remember this question is a change question, so make sure what you are writing about explains how far the UN's role in promoting human rights changed.

Answer

Here is a student response to the question. The teacher has made some comments. Rewrite the section where comments are made to improve it.

Good introduction. You have suggested that the UN's role in promoting human rights changed by it becoming more important.

Human rights have always been important to the UN. The UN Declaration of Human Rights was published in 1948. It could be argued that promoting human rights became even more important to the UN in the years 1991–2011.

Good paragraph. You have set out how the UN tried to promote human rights at the start of the period and have showed that its failure brought about one change.

Bosnia 1991–95 was a brutal war that involved different ethnic groups. It became an identity war, meaning some ethnic groups saw themselves as superior to others. The UN tried to protect human rights there through the UNHCR, which looked after refugees and provided humanitarian help. It also came up with the idea of 'safe areas' such as Srebrenica and Sarajevo where Bosnian Muslims (Bosniaks) could be protected from the Serbs who wanted to force them from their homes, which was against human rights. The safe areas did not work very well because the UN did not want to anger the Serbs, so their attacks on the safe areas often went unpunished. Finally in 1995 there was the Srebrenica massacre, when over 7,000 Bosniak men and boys were killed by the Serbs and Bosniak women and girls were raped. After this, the UN decided that it must promote human rights more forcefully, for example allowing NATO to bomb the Serbs.

This is a short paragraph but very useful as it gives a clear way in which the UN developed how it promoted human rights. It makes a good link to the next paragraph too.

After the Srebrenica massacre and another genocide in Rwanda, the UN Secretary-General said the UN had a duty to promote all human rights everywhere and in 2005 the UN had a summit that agreed if a country did not protect the human rights of all its people then the international community (the UN) must take action.

A little rushed? Two clear changes to the way in which the UN tried to promote human rights, however, and overall a good question focus.

In Sudan there was a huge human rights crisis especially in Darfur where the people were being killed and forced from their land by the Janjaweed, under orders from the Sudanese government. Sudan did not let the UN do much in Darfur other than protect humanitarian aid efforts. This was not enough but later it was agreed that the UN could work with the African Union. This was a change in how the UN promoted human rights because it was a joint operation, UNAMID. They tried to use the ICJ to arrest the leader of Sudan on war crimes as a way of promoting human rights but this didn't work.

A very rushed and brief paragraph. UNCIVPOL is a good idea to mention but needs to be developed a little. How useful is Iraq here?

Other ways in which the UN promoted human rights stayed the same, such as the work of the UNHCR. Also it got more involved in countries after peacekeeping missions to help human rights, like with UNCIVPOL. Sometimes this worked well. It could be said that the UN did not promote human rights by imposing sanctions on Iraq, although some say that human rights in Iraq were really bad anyway and the UN did nothing to promote them.

This is a disappointing conclusion. You have summarised in what ways there were changes, but not 'how far'. You need to make a judgement on the extent of the change. How much was there?

Overall the UN tried to promote human rights more actively and to intervene in countries when they weren't protecting the human rights of all their people. It came up with new ways to promote human rights such as safe areas (not successful) and UNCIVPOL and working with other organisations like the AU and ICJ. It also carried on using the UNHCR and other agencies, like before.

What are the strengths and weaknesses of this answer?
You can see the strengths and weaknesses of this answer from what the teacher says. The paragraphs on Bosnia and the short, but very focused one on the 2005 summit particularly helped this answer, although there were also some rushed sections.

GLOSSARY

38th parallel the line of latitude on a map that divides South Korea from North Korea

abstain to decide not to take part in something

administrative capital the place from where the business of running government is done

age of consent the word 'consent' means agreement; the term 'age of consent', however, means the age at which a person is old enough to lawfully agree to have sexual intercourse

aggressor a person or country that begins a fight or war with another person or country

alliance an arrangement in which two or more countries, groups etc. agree to work together to try to change or achieve something

amnesty an official pardon, especially for political offences

appease to give in to someone's demands in the hope that they will be satisfied and will demand no more

arbitrate to officially judge how an argument between two opposing sides should be settled. All sides agree on who is to judge on their dispute

armistice a legal and usually long-term agreement to stop fighting, but not to formally end the war. As of early 2017 there has been no formal end to the Korean War

article in this text, an article is a part of a law or legal agreement that deals with a particular point

boycotting refusing to buy something, use something, or take part in something as a way of protesting

ceasefire an agreement to stop fighting for a period of time, especially so that a more permanent agreement can be made

civil service the government departments that manage the affairs of the country

civil war a war in which opposing groups of people from the same country fight each other in order to gain political control

clan a large group of families who often share the same name

coalition a union of two or more political parties that allows them to form a government or fight an election together

compliance when someone obeys a rule, agreement or demand

conscription compulsory joining of the armed forces

contravention an action breaking an agreement or ruling

coup illegal seizure of power by the army, usually sudden and violent

covenant a formal, written agreement

defensive used or intended to protect someone or something against attack

delegate verb: to give part of your power or work to someone in a lower position than you; noun: someone who has been elected or chosen to speak, vote, or take decisions for a group

deploy to organise or move soldiers, military equipment etc so that they are in the right place and ready to be used

deportation compulsory removal of people to another country

dictator a ruler who has complete power over a country, especially one whose power has been gained by force

diplomacy the job or activity of managing the relationships between countries

disillusioned feeling let down or disappointed

dowry property and money that a woman gives to her husband when they marry in some societies

embargo an official order to stop trade with another country

epidemiological the study of the way diseases spread, and how to control them

ethnic origin/ethnicity the country, race, nation, tribe (and their customs and traditions) which someone comes from

execute either to kill someone, especially legally as a punishment or to do something that has been carefully planned

executive a body that has the power to carry something out, especially regarding political decisions or policies

factions groups within a larger organisation

federation a group of states forming one country, but each with independence over its own internal affairs

figurehead someone who seems to be the leader of a country or organisation but who has no real power

Great Depression the period during the 1930s when there was not much business activity and not many jobs; this led to a fall in trade and an increase in poverty, especially in countries with developed economies such as the USA, Japan, Germany and Britain

guerrilla warfare war fought by a small unofficial military group that fights in small groups

high treason the crime of acting against your country's interests and putting it in danger

Holocaust the systematised genocide of Jews by Nazi Germany, resulting in 6 million deaths

impartially in a fair or neutral way

implementation putting into practice, making happen

indicted brought to trial

intervention the act of becoming involved in an argument, fight, or other difficult situation in order to change what happens

liberate break free

mandate when one nation is put in the care and authority of another

mediator a person or organisation that tries to end a quarrel between two people, groups, countries, etc. by discussion

mercenaries professional soldiers who are hired to fight for whoever pays them, rather than fighting for a country

military liaison officer someone who gets different military organisations to work together

militia a group of people trained as soldiers, who are not part of the permanent army

nationalism strong loyalty to, and pride in, your country often making people see it as better than other nations

NATO The North Atlantic Treaty Organization (NATO) is a military and political alliance to safeguard the freedom and security of its member states

neutral not supporting any of the people or groups involved in an argument or disagreement

OSCE The Organization for Security and Co-operation in Europe; its aim is to promote regional security throughout Europe through political, social, environmental, humanitarian and military initiatives

partition the action of separating a country into two or more independent countries

people trafficking the buying and selling of people; the activity of taking people to another country and forcing them to work

political extremism a belief in making radical, possibly violent and illegal, changes in the way countries are governed

precondition something that must happen or exist before something else can happen

prime minister head of the government in many countries

ratify to sign or give formal agreement to a treaty

referendum when people vote to make a decision about a particular subject

reform a change or changes made to a system or organisation in order to improve it

remilitarise to bring a lot of soldiers and weapons back to an area from where they were removed

republic a country governed by elected representatives of the people, and led by a president, not a king or queen

revolution time when people change a ruler or political system by using force or violence; can also mean a complete change in ways of thinking, methods of working, etc.

right wing in politics, people and parties who support traditional ideas and do not like change

sanctions penalties or punishments; economic sanctions are ways of punishing a country by affecting its economy, such as stopping trading with it

sovereignty having supreme power; the right to govern

state benefits money given by the government to people who are poor, without a job, ill or need help and support

Sub-Saharan Africa the region of Africa that lies to the south of the Saharan desert

truce an agreement between enemies to stop fighting or arguing for a short time, or the period for which this is arranged

umbrella organisation an organisation created to bring together different groups and organisations that are working on the same issues; the umbrella organisation co-ordinates their activities and resources

unanimous agreed by everyone

unprecedented never having happened before

veto the power to reject something or prevent it from happening even though all other decision makers are in favour of it; can be a noun or a verb

violate to act against an official agreement, law or principle

warlord the leader of an unofficial military group fighting against a government, king or different group

weapons of mass destruction (WMDs) weapons able to indiscriminately kill large numbers of people. They include nuclear, chemical and biological weapons

INDEX